CREDIT CARDS

THE AUTHORITATIVE GUIDE

TO

CREDIT AND PAYMENT CARDS

First published 1994

British Library Cataloguing in Publication Data. A catalogue
record for this book is available from the British Library.

ISBN 0 948035 13 7

Published by:
Rushmere Wynne Ltd.
P.O. Box 491, Leighton Buzzard,
Bedfordshire LU7 7ZS

Printed by:
Redwood Books Ltd
Kennet house,
Kennet Way, Trowbridge,
Wiltshire BA14 9RN

CREDIT CARDS

THE AUTHORITATIVE GUIDE

TO

CREDIT AND PAYMENT CARDS

By

Ian Lindsey

Rushmere Wynne
England

CONTENTS

FOREWORD

When asked to write the Foreword to Ian's book, I looked into my wallet to see how many credit cards I carried. There were over a dozen, and there are many more which I use from time to time. It wasn't always like this, but I cannot remember not having, and enjoying the efficiency of, credit cards.

On a broader scale, credit cards of all kinds – cheque cards, cash cards, charge cards, debit cards and 'yes' credit cards – are one of the outstanding achievements of the banking industry. They have revolutionised personal finance and it is unlikely that the retailing explosion of the 1970s and 1980s could have happened without them. Their development has been the result of the innovation and marketing competence of bankers worldwide. And the technology needed to drive forward this progress has been the consequence of massive capital investment by the banks.

Given the pace of expansion, Ian's book is being published at an opportune time. Although, according to the author, the market for cards has reached an optimum level, around the corner lurks the integrated circuit card, likely to be the next main innovation of the credit card industry.

I think readers will benefit from this book and enjoy it. It is a concise and thorough review of the payment card sector, covering all its essential issues. For banking students, it offers a complete history, a full summary of card operations and an understanding of the profit and loss make–up of card companies. For the practising banker, the book provides an up–to–date assessment of the industry and a look into the future.

Ian Lindsey writes with the skill of an accomplished practitioner. The clarity of presentation is a tribute to his knowledge and humour (why was there a photograph of a gorilla on a card?). He is not afraid to speak his mind: the manipulation of the calculation of Annual Percentage Rates (APRs) is just one example he gives of areas where some members of the credit card industry need to reconsider their practices.

This book, written by the current Treasurer of the Chartered Institute of Bankers and a long–term member of its Council, is thus an important contribution to banking bibliography. I commend it to you without reservation.

Dr Andreas R. Prindl
President
The Chartered Institute of Bankers
Chairman
Nomura Bank International plc

INTRODUCTION

In 1983 Tony Drury, now the Managing Director of Rushmere Wynne Limited, wrote a book on the UK credit card market. Ten years later in 1993, I met Tony at a social gathering and suggested to him that there was a need to up–date his book. He nodded politely and turned to his drink!

However, a few weeks later Tony approached me and said he agreed that there was a need for an up–to–date book on UK payment/credit cards but he had been away from the market place so long that he was not competent to write it. He asked me to undertake the task for I had been involved with plastic more or less continuously since the launch of Access in the early 1970s.

We agreed that I would write a book aimed at professionals operating in the banking and financial services markets as well as academics, journalists and commentators on the plastic card scene. Given the many naive comments made by politicians, and indeed civil servants, on the subject of credit cards this book may prove most beneficial to them.

I would like to pay special thanks for the assistance I have received from Fiona Bawdon, who has undertaken a lot of the research, as well as to my deputy at Save & Prosper, Mark Christopher, for reading the draft and making many valuable comments which I have incorporated. I must also thank Hollis Fishelson–Holstine of Fair Isaacs for her most helpful contribution on the section devoted to credit scoring as well as to Patrick Nelson of Europay who insisted that I used the capital 'C' in the word MasterCard!

In these acknowledgements authors often pay tribute to their family for allowing them the time to write the book in the first place. I cannot do this for the first my wife and family knew that I had written a book was when the final draft was delivered to my home for proof reading. I had kept it a secret from them until that day.

Ian Lindsey
London
October 1994

ONE

WHAT IS A CREDIT CARD?

Most of us will be familiar with credit cards. Even if we don't hold them ourselves, we see them being used in shops and other retail outlets and being widely promoted through advertising. But what exactly is a credit card? The term is in fact used quite loosely but can be applied to a whole host of types of cards, backed by different organisations and used in different ways.

What is a Payment Card?

Credit and debit cards both fall into the category of **payment cards.** The main distinction between the two types is the account to which they relate. A **credit** card accesses a line of revolving credit (see below); whereas, a **debit** card usually accesses either a current account or a deposit account. From the point of view of making payments or obtaining cash, however, the two work in exactly the same way.

The first thing to notice about payment cards, credit or debit, is that they are made of plastic. This, however, may be set to change in the future. You may begin to see them made from other materials, such as metal, or perhaps from a substance which is more environmentally friendly than plastic.

Credit cards are a means whereby you can pay for goods and services and/or obtain cash. They may be issued by a financial institution, such as a bank or building society, or by other types of organisations, such as shops and fuel companies.

There will usually be a contract between the card issuer (say, a bank), and the cardholder (or customer), which sets out the rules for using the card. (Appendix Three shows a typical cardholder agreement). With bank-issued cards, there will always also be an agreement between a bank and the card acceptor, the outlet which agrees to accept the credit card as payment for its goods and services. This sets out the terms under which the cards will be accepted by the outlet. (Appendix Four shows a typical merchant agreement.)

Thus, with bank-issued cards, there are either three or four parties to the transaction: the cardholder (the customer); the card acceptor (the shop or service-provider), and the card issuer/merchant acquirer (the bank). Where the card–issuing bank and the merchant–acquiring bank are different, there are four parties to the transaction (see Table A on page 82) but where the card issuing bank and the merchant acquiring bank are the same, there are three parties to the transaction.

The two main bank-issued payment cards, and the ones that probably come to mind when most people think of the term "credit card", are VISA and MasterCard. With both of these types of card, it is a fundamental principle (as set out in their respective agreements) that card acceptors must honour all valid cards at all times. They cannot pick and choose. Clearly, the advantage of this for cardholders is that they know their card will be accepted wherever they see the VISA or MasterCard sign.

What does a Credit Card do?

Credit cards have three main functions (not all of which will apply to each type; see below).

They can be:
- a means of paying for goods and services;
- a means of obtaining cash;
- a source of revolving credit (see below).

Bank and building society-issued VISA and MasterCard cards allow the holder to pay for goods and services almost anywhere in the world. In some ways, they can be regarded as a form of international currency. While governments may be divided over the benefits or otherwise of a European-wide single currency, with credit cards, we effectively already have a currency that not only covers Europe but much of the rest of the world as well.

The bank issuing the credit card ensures that you can use your card almost anywhere in the world. It can be used to pay for goods in the currency of the country in which you happen to be, but you will be billed in sterling. The only disadvantage that credit cards have over a truly single European currency is the cost of converting your purchase in, say French francs, into the base currency, sterling. Normally, you would expect to pay a conversion fee of between 1-2 per cent above the wholesale or inter-bank rates of exchange.

The second function of credit cards is as a source of cash. This can be sterling, or almost any other currency in the world. You can get Russian roubles in Moscow or US$ out of a cash machine in Disneyland in America. Credit cards give you access to cash, 24 hours a day, 365 days a year, through the banks' cash dispenser operations which are linked via VISA and MasterCard.

Credit cards are also a source of revolving credit which works in a similar way to a bank overdraft. It simply means that the cardholder is allowed to effectively borrow money, up to a certain pre-set level, from the card issuer again and again. Once all or part of the amount is paid back, the cardholder has an automatic right to borrow again, up to his credit limit. It differs from a personal loan in that, with a loan, once the amount has been repaid, it can't be borrowed again without a new agreement.

Credit cards also differ from personal loans in that there is no fixed repayment programme, the borrower is not committed to paying back a certain amount over a certain period. The credit cardholder can pay back the debt over a timescale and by amounts that suit him. If he prefers, he can maintain the debt indefinitely, simply paying the minimum monthly amount, usually 5 per cent of the outstanding balance and then borrowing again the 5 per cent repaid.

Types of Card

As mentioned earlier, when talking of "credit cards", most people will think of the familiar bank-issued cards, VISA and MasterCard. But there are many other types which fall under the generic heading of credit card.

Bank-issued cards

Although the issuing banks generally give these cards a brand name, such as Access or Barclaycard, bank-issued cards are usually linked to either the MasterCard or VISA organisations. VISA and MasterCard are bank-owned payment organisations which facilitate the exchange and settlement of transactions (see Chapter Three). If you look on a credit card, you are likely to find either a VISA or a MasterCard logo. There may also be the logo for Europay, which is the business partner of MasterCard in Europe (again, this is explained in more detail in Chapter Three).

To join VISA or MasterCard, the card-issuing organisation has to be either a bank or a building society. This would cover any organisation which is set up under a country's commercial banking laws, and which is authorised to accept demand deposits. In the UK, this covers all banks authorised by the Bank of England and building societies which fall under the auspices of the Building Societies Commissioner. Non–banks cannot join VISA or MasterCard and, hence, the development of co–branded and affinity cards as explained below.

Charge Cards

The two main charge cards are American Express (known as Amex) and Diners. Charge cards are similar to bank-issued cards in that they are a means to pay for goods and services at most places in the world; and you can use them to obtain cash. That is where, however, the similarity ends. Unlike with a bank-issued card, the period of credit is limited. The debt on the card must be repaid in full, monthly, or charges will be incurred. You do not have the choice of whether or not to take extended credit.

This means that, unlike the bank issuers, Amex and Diners do not have interest income on which to rely. As a result, they have quite substantial joining and annual card fees and also charge the card acceptor, the shop or merchant, fairly high fees.

Charge cards are accepted in far fewer places than the major bank cards, tending to be restricted to business and tourist areas.

JCB

The JCB card is issued by the Japan Credit Bureau and is developing into an international payments card, aimed at the very wealthy. In the UK, the Midland Bank has arrangements with JCB to acquire transactions at selected merchants. Like most Japanese enterprises, the JCB card is likely to have a long gestation period and then emerge rapidly as a serious market force.

Gold Cards

Gold cards function in exactly the same way as any other payment card. You can use them to pay for goods and services and to obtain cash. However, there are many different types of gold card, depending on which bank issued the card. What they all have in common is that they are generally aimed at the card issuer's more affluent customers, who usually have a greater need for flexibility in their financial transactions.

A gold card will operate either as a credit card or a charge card, depending on which bank is the issuer. For example, Barclays Premier VISA Card operates as a charge card, but brings with it a separate bank account, usually with an unsecured overdraft facility of up to £10,000. Save & Prosper issues a gold card which is a deferred debit card. In this case, transactions are debited directly to the holder's current account and each item will show up separately on his monthly bank statement, alongside cheques, standing order and direct debit payments.

There will usually, but not always, be a charge for a gold card. Exceptions to this are the Co-op Bank, which issues its cards without charge; and

Flemings/S&P, which charges a monthly fee only where customers have less than £2,500 in their account when their statements are prepared.

American Express also issues a platinum card, which is an upmarket version of its gold card. Recently, bankers Coutts & Co have issued a Signia card, linked to Eurocard/MasterCard, with a £30,000 monthly spending limit but with an annual fee of £250.

Co-branded Cards

Co-branded cards are where a bank promotes jointly a credit card with another, non-financial, institution. In the early 1980s, Barclays issued a co–branded card with British Airways, which was unsuccessful and subsequently withdrawn. In the mid–1980s, Bank of Scotland issued a co–branded card with the Automobile Association. This card is still operating, although it does not appear to be promoted actively.

Co-branding with motor manufacturers is a phenomena which began in the United States some two or three years ago and which has recently spread to the UK. In 1993, we saw the launch in this country of the GM credit card (backed by car manufacturer General Motors and HFC Trust), which has been followed more recently by Ford Barclaycard (backed by car manufacturer Ford and Barclays Bank). There is, however, an important distinction between these two cards in that HFC Trust is a "silent" brand on the GM card, whereas neither Ford nor Barclaycard are "silent" in the Ford Barclaycard. The latter is probably the only true example of co–branding in the UK.

Cardholders use their co-branded cards in the same way they would any bank-issued card, but each time they make a purchase, they are accumulating points which will allow them to claim a discount on the price of buying a new car from the participating manufacturer. Generally, the bank issues the card and bears the credit risk, and the car manufacturer provides the discount. The attractions for the car manufacturer are increased sales and customer loyalty.

Ford and GM have had some considerable success with their cards in the US, and clearly hope for a repetition here. However, they may have overlooked the fact that the scope for participants may be less in the UK, where more than 50 per cent of new cars are bought by companies for their employees. However, the points can be collected for discounts towards company cars so that company car users also have an incentive to participate in these discount schemes.

The *Sunday Times* has launched a co-branded VISA card with the Bank of Scotland. Again, the Bank of Scotland is a "silent" brand. The card brings with it a number of special offers, including free copies of the *Sunday Times*. The *Express* card is issued in association with Flemings/S&P and Express Newspapers and provides a low interest rate but no special offers.

Affinity Cards

Affinity cards are issued by banks and linked to a particular group of people or organisation. For example, graduates of Nottingham University have been invited to apply for a card issued by the Bank of Scotland. The card carries an illustration of the university, which will receive an income from the bank related to the amount each cardholder spends using the card.

Affinity cards can be aimed at groups both large and small, ranging from, say, 5,000 people up to two million. Generally, the larger the affinity group the lower the actual affinity and the less likelihood of members applying for the card. The smaller the group, the greater the loyalty is likely to be and so the greater the chance of members wanting a card.

Store Cards

Store, or shop-issued cards, need to be treated separately. Unlike with other credit cards, it is not normally a three-or-four-way transaction, but a two-way arrangement: the card issuer is normally the card acceptor.

By and large, store cards cannot be used internationally. The card can usually be used in shops within the store group only. They also have fewer uses than other cards: they are a means or payment and a source of credit, but you cannot usually use them to obtain cash.

From the stores' point of view, these cards are seen primarily as a means of increasing sales and building customer loyalty. Stores will expect to make a profit from their cards, but the prime objective is to build up a client database and to encourage shoppers to come back.

Store cards tend to attract younger customers and are more widely available than bank-issued cards. The criteria for their issue tend to be more lax. Quite simply, someone could be granted £1,000 credit on a store card but would be turned down for a similar amount by, say, Access. With the exception of the store groups John Lewis and Marks & Spencer, store cards tend to operate on the basis of higher interest rates, larger margins and higher credit losses.

Electronic Debit Cards

Although debit cards, like Switch and VISA Delta, are not strictly credit cards, if they are used in conjunction with a bank overdraft, they provide access to revolving credit in the same way as a credit card.

Telephone Cards

There are two types of telephone card: pre-payment cards (where you buy a card giving you a certain number of telephone-call units), which are not strictly credit cards; and British Telecom's credit card. BT's credit card allows you to make calls from a public phone box, the cost of which are then added to your home or business telephone bill. BT also issues credit cards which can be used to phone your home number only where, again, the cost is added to your telephone bill.

Fuel Cards

Fuel cards are issued by petrol companies, primarily to operators of company car fleets for distribution to their drivers. These cards allow the holder access to credit in order to buy petrol, the cost of which may then subsequently be met by their employer.

Mondex Card

The Mondex card is a prepayment card which will be issued on a trial basis in Swindon in 1995. The word Mondex is an amalgam of 'monde' the French for world and 'ex' for exchange.

Between 80% and 90% of transactions worldwide are made in cash. Cash is expensive to handle and the risk of loss is relatively high. Mondex enables the instant transmission of value with a high level of security.

Mondex value can be transmitted down a telephone line – unlike cash. Transactions do not need the intervention of third parties, such as banks, or validation. There is no need for signature checking or other validation so that value can be transferred instantaneously from one Mondex card to another. The payments are conditional on the payer card having sufficient value for the payment and the receiving card accepting the payment after checking the authority of the paying card.

In effect the chips in the two cards are programmed to check each other out. The actual data is encrypted for the actual transfer which virtually eliminates the possibility of unauthorised interference.

Mondex has been developed by National Westminster Bank PLC. It has been licensed to Midland Bank and British Telecom. NatWest is now marketing the service globally. **It could revolutionise payment systems worldwide.**

TWO

THE BENEFITS OF PAYMENT CARDS

To the card user

Flexibility and convenience at home and abroad

Perhaps the overwhelming benefits to the user of a payment card are the convenience and flexibility it brings over cash, or some other means of paying. This is true particularly for anyone who travels abroad – whether on holiday or for business reasons.

Payment cards, particularly VISA, MasterCard, and to a lesser extent Amex and Diners, are widely accepted around the world. This means that when you are planning a trip abroad, you may not need to organise large amounts of foreign currency or travellers cheques before you go – you can simply rely on your payment card instead, with perhaps a small amount of currency for taxi fares and the inevitable gratuities.

Less time-consuming and better value than travellers' cheques

Payment cards have many advantages over travellers' cheques or currency, before, during and after your trip abroad. With travellers' cheques, you have to decide how much you are likely to spend in advance, order them a few days before you go (and remember to collect them), and pay for them upfront. This latter point effectively means that, until you actually spend the cheques, you are giving the issuing bank the free use of your money.

When you come back from your trip, unless you have planned your expenditure with unusual precision, you are likely to have currency or cheques left over. You then have the choice of queuing at the bank all over again, and paying a fee to convert your cheques back to sterling, or retaining them in the hope that you will remember to take them with you the next time you go away. Where the amounts involved are small, many people will prefer to keep the cheques and avoid paying additional commission and the almost-inevitable loss on the exchange rate. The upshot of this is that you will be extending your credit to the bank for a protracted period – possibly even indefinitely. Although the amounts in individual cases may be small, the sums can add up to be substantial. Standard Chartered Bank, for example, is said to be sitting on around £800m-worth of uncashed travellers' cheques – money which has come out of its travelling customers' pockets. Even when interest rates are only, say, 5 per cent, this would produce some £40m income a year for Standard Chartered.

Using a payment card during trips abroad is, by contrast, a very straight-forward process. There is no need to pre-plan or pre-budget, which frees you to make spontaneous purchases (which might be outside the scope of your travellers' cheques), and to change your arrangements at the last minute, staying on for an extra few days if you so choose. There is no need to pay in advance; your account will only be debited once you have actually made your expenditure. Furthermore, the exchange rate you pay with your payment card is likely to be more competitive than that for travellers' cheques and currency. As well as saving money, payment cards can represent enormous savings in time – time spent not having to queue in a bank before, during and after a trip.

Automatic and instant credit

The ability to make spontaneous purchases is, obviously, a benefit to cardholders when they are at home, as well as abroad. But whether purchases are planned in advance or not, payment cards are an automatic source of credit which may save the holder from having to visit his or her bank to ask for a loan. Many people still feel intimidated about seeing their bank manager and value the fact that payment cards are impersonal (your application can be handled through the post) as a distinct advantage.

Consumer protection

Under section 75 of the Consumer Credit Act 1974, customers are provided with extra protection covering goods costing between £100 and £15,000 bought on credit cards. If the goods that you have paid for turn out to be sub-standard, or fail to be delivered, you can claim compensation from the card-issuing bank (see Chapter Eight for more details).

There are, however, limits to what may be covered by this Act. At Save & Prosper, a 66-year-old male customer came to their offices unsuccessfully demanding a refund after using his credit card to join a dating agency, where none of the women turned out to be to his liking. In another unsuccessful case, a customer asked for a refund because he was not happy with the time–share property he had bought, unseen, in Portugal. He had been assured that the property was sea-facing, which it was. However, it was positioned some seven miles inland.

Discounts and bonuses

Cardholders may also be eligible for discounts on a whole host of services: private health care plans, such as PPP and BUPA, car breakdown services, wine and holiday clubs, for example. Some card issuers also run schemes where you accumulate points each time you use the card, which can later be exchanged for goods, as set out in a catalogue supplied by the issuer. The Barclays Profiles scheme is, perhaps, the leading UK example of a points scheme. NatWest offers Air Miles as an incentive.

Free insurance cover

There are also a number of substantial "hidden" benefits to some payment cards, of which holders may often be unaware. Credit cards occasionally bring with them their own insurance cover where goods or services have been paid for with the card. This cover falls into three categories:

- Replacement of goods
  If an item you have paid for with your card is lost, damaged or stolen within three months of buying it, some card issuers, particularly Amex and Barclaycard, will pay for a replacement.

- Travel accident insurance
  You are automatically covered for death or serious injury if your travel has been paid for with your card. In some cases this may mean a pay-out of up to £0.25m. This would, obviously, cover, say, an accident during travel, but would also encompass your commuting to work, if you paid for your season ticket with your payment card.

- Travel delay insurance
  If your travel arrangements are held up for any reason, some card issuers will pay you compensation.

Access to cash

The credit card cash-dispenser network effectively means that cardholders have instant access to cash anywhere in the world, all day, everyday.

Disadvantages

There is, of course, a price to pay for all the benefits of payment cards listed above. Cardholders are increasingly being charged an annual fee and the rates of interest incurred, if outstanding amounts are not paid back immediately, may be high compared with, say, that charged on an overdraft. However, this is not always the case.

To the card acceptor

Guaranteed payment

Payment cards have considerable advantages over cheques for the retailer. If, say, a shop does not take credit cards, and a customer wants to pay by cheque for an item which costs more than his cheque guarantee limit (and many of them are still set at £50), the shop faces a difficult choice. Either accept the cheque for the higher amount and risk it being bounced by the bank, or turn down a potential sale.

Increased sales

It is argued by the card-issuing bank that accepting payment cards can boost sales. They claim that it allows customers to make spontaneous purchases, that they otherwise would not be able to make. This, however, is probably less of a factor now that so many outlets accept payment cards. In the days when there were far fewer of them, to be the only shop on the high-street taking, say VISA, may have given the retailer a competitive edge.

Immediate value

When a merchant pays the credit card vouchers he has received into the bank, normally they are treated as cash, and immediately credited to his account. This has clear cash-flow advantages over cheques, which will usually take at least three days to clear. However, some banks are now attempting to delay the availability of cleared funds if the credit card transactions are not electronic.

Greater security

Although credit card transactions have the immediacy of cash when they are paid into the merchant's bank account, before they reach the bank, they have the advantages of cheques, in that they are virtually thief-proof. A till filled with thousands of pounds worth of cash may be tempting to dishonest staff or other thieves. Whereas a till full of thousands of pounds worth of credit card vouchers is unlikely to be raided. The vouchers are of little use to anyone other than the named card acceptor.

Speed of transactions at the point of sale

In the old days, processing a credit card payment at the point of sale could be a time-consuming and fiddly business – taking far longer than simply counting cash. However, as cash registers have become more sophisticated, the opposite may be true.

Now that an increasing number of stores and other outlets use EFTPOS (electronic funds transfer at the point of sale) equipment, the magnetic stripe of a payment card is simply run through the till, which may make it quicker than a cash transaction.

The EFTPOS system speeds up the process beyond the point of sale as well. It means the card acceptor can supply his sales information electronically to the card issuer – which saves the bank having to deal with a paper-based system. Some merchants are already beginning to argue that, where information is supplied to banks in this easier-to-handle form, they ought to qualify for a reduction in the charges they have to pay to the card issuer.

Disadvantages

As touched on above, a bone of contention between card acceptors and card issuers is over cost. Many retailers object to paying a merchant service fee, which is around 1.6 per cent of the value of the transaction in the case of UK bank-issued cards, and as much as 3-4 per cent for Amex.

To the issuer

Profit

The first benefit to issuers is that payment cards are a source of profit for their business. They generate income from the merchant service fee (mentioned above), from card fees and interest charges paid by cardholders and from cross-selling other banking and investment services (see below).

Worldwide service

By being a member of, say, VISA or MasterCard, the smallest bank in the world can provide its clients with an international payment mechanism, which is identical to that of its bigger rivals. For example, each day, Flemings/Save & Prosper, is given one amount by VISA of all the credit card transactions it has to settle among all the participating banks around the world. It then has to make just one transaction, paying over that amount to VISA, which then proceeds to distribute it to the banks entitled to receive it. After profit, this ability to provide a worldwide service is probably the biggest benefit to a card issuer.

Greater efficiency

By encouraging its customers to use payment cards, banks are likely to have to deal with fewer transactions by cheque. This has a number of advantages.

The daily information supplied by, say, VISA and MasterCard comes in electronic form, which makes debiting the appropriate amount from customers' accounts, a quick and simple process. Cheque payments, by contrast, are relatively expensive to process.

Cross-selling opportunities

Anyone who uses a credit card will get a monthly statement from his or her bank. This gives the bank the opportunity every single month to promote other services – such as investment or insurance products – to its existing customers. This can be a highly-effective marketing tool. At Flemings/Save & Prosper, some 30 per cent of its credit card customers have bought other services at one time or another.

Customer inertia

Bank and payment card customers do not tend to shop around for these services. Once people have a bank account or a credit card, it is rare for them to switch to a rival organisation. This, therefore, gives banks the chance to charge relatively high rates of interest on credit card use without fearing that it will drive away customers in their thousands. In this way, credit cards can be a good profit source for the bank.

Cross-subsidisation

The relatively high rates of return available because of customer inertia (see above), mean that these credit card profits can be used to subsidise other, less lucrative, areas of business. Most banks would admit to making losses on their current account business, particularly when interest rates are low. They may, however, be able to swallow these losses by off-setting them against above-average profits from credit card business.

Should customers be objecting to such cross-subsidisation? Some may feel there is no real need to be concerned. Those with credit cards will also have current accounts and what they lose on the former they gain on the latter. However, not all current account holders have credit cards. It is thus this group of people who are winning from the banks' current arrangements. The cost to the banks of running these customers' current accounts at a loss, may be being met by its credit cardholders.

Economic issues

Perhaps surprisingly for something which is so familiar to all of us, the way credit cards are used can also have a significant impact on the wider economy of the country.

When a credit card is simply used as a means of payment – rather than a source of credit – and the debt is cleared at the end of each month, it has no impact on the economy at all. The transaction can be seen simply as replacing cash or bank deposits as a means of payment. However, where the balance outstanding is not cleared in full, these sums could be argued to add to the total borrowings in the UK.

In 1993, the total amount of money outstanding on credit cards was some £9.164bn, of which 69 per cent, that is £6.323bn, was earning interest. However, this figure represented approximately only 4-5 per cent of the country's total lending to the personal sector. It can be argued, therefore, that credit card lending has a minimal impact on the economy as a whole.

Unused credit

Credit card customers on average are borrowing around 40 per cent of their credit limit. This unused 60 per cent represents in total a huge amount of credit which, in theory, could be entered into the economic equation. If it were, it could lead to an increase in the money supply, with consequent increases in consumer demand and a rise in the rate of inflation. However, compared with the total level of consumer borrowing, the credit card element is relatively small and so unlikely to have a significant impact on the UK economy.

As well as the wider economic implications, this unused credit also has cost implications for the issuing bank. It is obliged to provide capital to fund this level of borrowing should it ever be required.

Government regulation

The economic implications of credit cards mean that, from time to time, governments have sought to intervene in the relationship between cardholder and card issuer.

In 1973, the UK economy was in a mess. In an attempt to meet requirements imposed by the International Monetary Fund, which was helping to bail out the UK, the Labour government increased the minimum monthly repayment on credit cards from 5 per cent of the total outstanding to 15 per cent. However, moves of this kind can only have limited success. On this occasion, some credit cardholders simply could not afford to make the higher payment. The banks were left with the choice of continuing to accept payments of 5 per cent, or bankrupting their customers and, not surprisingly, chose the former.

THREE

BANK AND NON–BANK CARDS

VISA

VISA International Service Association (from where the VISA name is derived) is a non-stock (that is, it has no shares), non-profit-making company, registered in Delaware USA. It is owned and controlled by its members, through five elected regional boards, which in turn nominate directors to sit on the VISA International board.

The five regions are:

- USA

- Canada

- Latin America

- Europe, Middle East and Africa (EMEA)

- Asia Pacific

The boards representing each of these regions are run democratically. Elections for EMEA regional directors are held every two years, and votes are allocated to member organisations according to the proportion of business each puts through the VISA organisation. What this means, in effect, is that an organisation, say, the size of Barclays has sufficient volume to automatically appoint a member on a VISA regional board; whereas smaller companies will have to rely on the votes of their competitors. However, two places on each board are reserved for representatives from smaller companies, to ensure that the interests of smaller banks are represented with one director being elected on the basis of one member, one vote.

As we have said, each regional board in turn nominates directors to the 25-strong VISA International board. Again, the number of directors each region gets on the international board will depend on the proportion of business it contributes to the total turnover of VISA as a whole. For example, the regions of the USA and

Europe, Middle East and Africa, have similar turnover volume and both are able to nominate seven directors to the international board.

VISA currently operates an open membership policy. This means that any bank or building society which is organised under the commercial laws (or equivalent) in any country, and is authorised to accept demand deposits (deposits which can be withdrawn without notice, normally by cheque) is likely to be accepted so long as it can put up a reasonable business plan.

The upshot of VISA's approach to new members is that it currently has around 40 member banks in the UK. This compares with around 30 bank members of MasterCard in the UK (see below) which, up until the mid 1980s, effectively had a closed membership policy in the UK.

The VISA organisation has three main functions:

- It exists to promote – and protect – the VISA name as an international brand, which is accepted and recognised throughout the world. To this end of promoting the uniformity of the brand-name, normally, there has been no visible distinction between the appearance of a VISA debit or a VISA credit card. However, recently VISA introduced the Delta brand as a debit card, although members are not compelled to use this brand on their debit cards. In general, the Delta brand is used by UK VISA debit card issuing banks only.

- It is an international clearing house for financial transactions. Just as the banks use the Bankers Clearing House for cheques, so VISA is a means of authorising and transmitting financial transactions – both on a national and an international basis, with around 7 billion being handled in 1993. As with the clearing system, VISA members are required to make just a single payment to settle the day's international transactions.

- As well as being a means of transmitting transactions, VISA is also a means of settling those transactions. Although these two functions are clearly linked, they should be thought of separately. The international currency of VISA – the one in which international transactions are settled – is the US$. For example, if you make a purchase in Paris in French Francs, it will be settled by the card-issuing bank with VISA in US$. For domestic transactions, however, settlement will usually be made in the host country's currency – so, anything bought by a UK cardholder in this country, would be settled in Sterling. It is a maxim of the organisation that a VISA card is a VISA card is a VISA card: it matters not for settlement purposes whether it is a VISA credit or debit card.

It is also important to realise what VISA does not do. It does not issue cards; it does not have a direct relationship with the cardholder; it does not recruit merchants to accept VISA cards for payment of goods and services. All of these are functions of the member banks.

MASTERCARD

The structure of MasterCard International Inc (hereafter referred to as MasterCard) has several similarities to that of VISA (see above). It is a company registered in the USA; it is non-profit-making and is controlled by the membership. It has a number of regions, which mirror those of VISA, except that Europe is treated separately from the region made up by the Middle East and Africa.

Like VISA, MasterCard is a non-stock company. However, its position is more complicated by the fact that MasterCard bought a 12.247 per cent shareholding in Eurocard International which later became Europay International (see below) and has now delegated to Europay responsibility for its activities in the UK, Eire and Continental Europe.

The board structure of MasterCard appears to be less democratic than that of VISA. Membership of its board is by nomination, although there is a formal election at the annual meeting of MasterCard at which all eligible members are able to vote on the basis of business volume. Europay is a company with shares, and the board are able to nominate their MasterCard directors. There are 29 MasterCard directors of whom one is from the UK and a further five are from Continental Europe, fewer than VISA. Nor, at MasterCard, does there appear to be any special provision for representing the interests of smaller members.

Despite the differences in set-up between MasterCard and VISA, the functions are broadly the same:

- To promote and protect its family of brands, namely MasterCard, Maestro and Cirrus.

- To provide a means of authorising and transmitting transactions.

- To provide a means of settling transactions worldwide.

Like VISA, MasterCard does not issue cards nor does it recruit merchants. These are within the province of the member banks. It is quite usual for banks to be members of both VISA and MasterCard, where they will be referred to as "dual" banks.

Europay

Europay, as we have said (see above), is an independent company which is the European business partner of MasterCard. It is a fairly new organisation, which was created out of the merger between Eurocard and eurocheque. Eurocard was a European charge card operation which had the organisation eurocheque working alongside it, albeit independently. Although both companies were separate from one another, they did have strong links. They jointly owned European Payment System Services (EPSS), a Brussels-based company, used for the computer processing of their transactions: many directors were common to both companies.

In September 1992, the two organisations were merged to become Europay International. Europay oversees the activities of Eurocard and eurocheque is the European agent of MasterCard. All MasterCard's European activities, including those in the UK and Eire, now have to be channelled through Europay.

Europay is non-profit-making but, unlike MasterCard, it is a company with shareholders. Europay's shareholders are European banks and, of course, MasterCard International. It does, of course, budget for a small surplus as do VISA and MasterCard. Europay's shareholders are the banks, which nominate directors to the board. In the UK, the Access consortium (see below) took a 15 per cent share in Eurocard in April 1978, which entitled it to nominate two directors to the Eurocard board, which subsequently became the Europay board. The Access shareholding has since been transferred to the new organisation, called MasterCard/Europay UK Limited.

Europay International is based in Waterloo, Belgium and has regional offices in London and six other European cities. It manages the Eurocard, MasterCard, eurocheque, Maestro and Cirrus brands in Europe.

Most of the banks which now issue MasterCard payment cards, including all the Access banks (see below), own shares in MasterCard/Europay UK Limited. In turn, that company owns 12.247 per cent of Europay Limited. MasterCard/Europay UK is an organisation which co-ordinates non-competitive issues between the UK MasterCard banks, such as fraud prevention. The UK banks still nominate two directors to the board of the Europay, thereby representing the majority views of the UK banks.

Europay also has five advisory committees – made up of senior European bankers supported by Europay International staff. The committees cover marketing, operations, security, fraud and technical matters.

An easy way of thinking about the somewhat complicated links between MasterCard and Europay, which may help your understanding of the relationship, is that Europay is the equivalent of VISA's regional operation for Europe. Europay is seen by some UK bankers as being dominated by the north European banks.

Up until quite recently, there was considerable resistance among banks in some European countries towards payment cards. During the early 1980s, in Germany, in particular, the banks wanted nothing to do with these cards, largely because they had invested heavily in the eurocheque service. They perceived VISA and MasterCard to be dominated by the USA, and resisted any attempts to sign up with these card organisations. Furthermore, eurocheques have been extremely profitable for the banks – with them receiving a commission of 1.65 per cent of the value of each currency cheque written.

Eventually, however, MasterCard persuaded Eurocard to enter into an alliance. Under this agreement, MasterCard effectively delegated all of its activities in Europe to Eurocard. It is possible that the Continental European banks in particular now recognise that payment cards may ultimately replace the use of eurocheques.

ACCESS

All Access cards are MasterCards – but not all MasterCards are Access cards.

Access is a brand name which appears on most UK-issued MasterCards, although not on any cards issued in other countries.

The Access scheme was originally launched by the UK banks Lloyds, Midland, National Westminster, and The Royal Bank of Scotland in 1972. The four banks owned the Joint Credit Card Company Limited (JCCC), which employed sales staff to recruit merchants who would accept Access cards. They also shared common computer processing facilities operated by the JCCC. Each bank was, however, responsible for issuing its own cards and bearing the credit and fraud losses on these cards.

In April 1975, Access affiliated to the Interbank Card Association, later Mastercharge, now MasterCard, allowing for full reciprocity on cardholders and merchants worldwide. Access cards obtained international acceptability.

Then in the 1980s, the arrangements between the Access consortium banks began to break up. The banks decided to compete with each other by recruiting and servicing merchants on an individual basis. The move was the direct result of the UK move towards duality, which started when Lloyds put in an application to join VISA and subsequently began issuing a VISA debit card. It also put sales people on the road to recruit merchants to take both MasterCard and VISA.

The second stage of the break–up of the banks' consortium came when the Access transaction processing operations were hived off into a new company called Signet. The banks later sold this operation to First Data Resources (see below), which now undertakes credit card processing for Lloyds, Midland,

NatWest and the Royal Bank. It also handles transactions for a number of smaller banks and building societies.

The banks also recognised the asset they held in terms of the Access name. To optimise the marketing advantage the name conferred, they set up Access Brand Limited, owned by Lloyds, Midland, NatWest, Royal Bank and Bank of Ireland, with the sole purpose of promoting the Access brand in the UK.

It is generally recognised, however, that the Access name may ultimately decline as the MasterCard brand becomes more prevalent in this country. Although Access is well known in the UK, MasterCard has the tremendous advantage of being a worldwide branding. Access is really just a domestic brand.

AMERICAN EXPRESS

American Express (Amex) is a company which operates independently of the major banks. It does, however, sometimes enter into alliances with the banks. For example, Lloyds issues a Gold Amex card where the customer has an account with Amex, but also an associated account with Lloyds which provides an overdraft facility. In general, however, where an Amex card is issued, there will be no association with the banks and will, in fact, be in competition with them.

There are three types of Amex card. These are the familiar standard green card; the gold card, which is an up–market version; and, for the very seriously rich, the platinum card. Amex does not publicise its criteria for issuing platinum cards but there are estimated to be only around 1,000 of them throughout the world.

Amex has not made significant progress in the UK in the last 10 to 15 years. It has been hampered by the recognition among UK consumers that the mass market cards issued by banks and building societies perform most of the functions of an Amex card and are considerably cheaper. VISA and MasterCards have other advantages in that they are more widely accepted than are Amex cards – which tend to be restricted to the major tourist and business centres.

One reason why Amex cards are accepted at fewer outlets than other payment cards is the higher costs involved. Normally, Amex cards are more expensive both to card acceptors and cardholders. The reason for this is largely because, as a charge (rather than credit) card, Amex does not receive interest income from cardholders. It has, therefore, just two sources of income, the card joining and membership fees paid by cardholders; and the merchant service fees paid by card acceptors. These latter charges are particularly high, at around 3-4 per cent of the sales value, compared with less than 2 per cent for bank-issued cards.

To try to overcome this difficulty, Amex has launched its Optima card. Holders of Amex cards can apply for an Optima credit card, which is intended to have a lower rate of interest than that of the major banks. In this country, however, the Optima card appears generally to have failed to take off. One reason for this may be the fact that cardholders need to obtain an Amex Green or Gold card, with all its associated joining and annual fees, before being able to apply for an Optima card.

Amex cards do have two advantages. An Amex card, by virtue of its advertising campaigns, conveys status on the cardholder; and it provides a level of service and expenditure information breakdown which is not being matched by the banks. This latter point can make Amex cards particularly attractive to companies seeking to issue payment cards to their employees, as they are more easily able to analyse spending patterns.

As well as operating its own charge card, Amex also owned a subsidiary company which handles the processing of many of the major credit cards. In 1986, it set up First Data Resources (FDR) in the UK, which subsequently bought Signet (see above) from the Access banks. However, in the early 1990s, Amex floated more than 50 per cent of its stake in FDR, so indirectly, Amex earns income from processing transactions for its rivals. It is expected that eventually Amex will dispose of its entire stake in FDR.

DINERS CLUB INTERNATIONAL

Like Amex, Diners Club is a charge card which does not normally offer extended credit. It is sold to customers on the basis of the status it conveys and service. In the UK, the Diners franchise is operated by Citibank Diners Club Europe which is a division and trading style of Citibank International plc. The 1992 accounts for Diners Club Limited show that the company made an operating loss, before taxation, of £1.3m, which was less than the £3.5m lost in 1991. Diners is thought to have moved back into profit during 1993.

Along with Amex, Diners has suffered from competition both from VISA and MasterCard. Potential clients have realised that VISA cards and MasterCards are more generally accepted than Diners, and considerably less expensive.

In recent years, Diners has concentrated on a joint marketing agreement with British Airways, in which BA corporate customers book travel, accommodation and restaurants on their BA/Diners Club card. Around 40,000 of Diners' 300,000 UK-based customers have these joint cards.

NON-BANK CARDS

Store cards

There are three different categories of store card, and sometimes shops will offer more than one type.

- Option account. This operates like a bank-issued credit card (except it can be used only in the issuing store group). The cardholder will be given a credit limit and receive monthly statements of expenditure on the card. He or she can pay off the entire amount outstanding each month, or just pay a minimum monthly sum.

- Budget account. The holder pays a fixed amount to the store each month and his or her credit limit is calculated as a multiple of this amount. For example, if £50 a month is paid, the cardholder may be able to spend up to, say, 12 or 24 times that amount.

- Charge card account. This works like any other type of charge card. The holder can use the card to pay for goods and services provided by the store group and has to settle the outstanding amount in full each month.

The market in store cards falls into two broad areas: those companies, like John Lewis (see below), which impose fairly stringent controls over the granting of credit facilities and which offer relatively competitive rates of interest; and those whose cards are more freely granted (sometimes simply on the basis that the customer already has a cheque guarantee card) and which charge far higher interest rates, sometimes up to around 30 per cent.

Particularly during the boom times of the late 1980s, some store groups seemed content to run their credit card arrangements as loss-makers. They saw the cards as a means of building customer loyalty and increasing sales of the goods they supplied and were prepared to take reasonably high credit losses (which were, to some extent, offset by relatively high interest rates).

Marks & Spencer

Marks & Spencer, the high-street shop chain, launched its payment card in 1984. The store does not publicise much information about its card, although it is generally believed to operate at a profit. M&S has around 2,625,000 accounts and, because some of these will have more than one card issued, say for spouses, 3,470,000 cardholders.

Although it is called a "charge card", the M&S card is, in fact, a credit card. The rationale for the launch of its own card was to avoid paying the merchant service charges that go with accepting bank-issued cards and to build up a base of loyal customers. M&S stores do not, at present, accept any other charge or credit cards, although it has now agreed to accept Switch debit cards and VISA Delta.

The philosophy behind the M&S charge card appears to be something of a departure from that which drives its other products, such as clothes and foodstuffs. Generally speaking, M&S has developed for itself a reputation of providing excellent quality products at a reasonably competitive price. Its goods may not be the cheapest available on the high street, but because they are of such high quality, they represent good value for money. It is less clear, however, that its charge card is such a "good buy".

The M&S charge card does not seem to adhere to this philosophy of giving "extra quality" over comparable available items (the cards can only be used in M&S stores) – yet the customer is still being charged a premium price for the product. The interest rates charged by M&S for credit may be lower than those for many store cards (see below); but they are significantly less competitive than those charged by, say, the store group John Lewis and for bank-issued cards (which have the "added value" of being able to be much more widely used).

John Lewis

The store group John Lewis introduced its Option Account – which operates as a traditional credit card, allowing customers to run it as a monthly account or to have a period of extended credit – in 1985. The group, however, has a long history of offering credit, but its previous arrangements have been consolidated into the Option Account.

John Lewis's rationale for its Option Account is similar to that of M&S for its charge card: to build customer loyalty, and to avoid paying the relatively high charges incurred for accepting bank-issued cards. It does not accept any bank-issued credit cards, but it does accept Switch and VISA Delta cards.

Like M&S, John Lewis does not publicise much information about its credit operations. However, according to figures published by the group, in November 1990, it had around 1.2 million cards issued, or 8 per cent of the store card market.

John Lewis has one of the most competitive interest rates available for a store card – and some of the strictest credit controls. Credit is not granted automatically (say, on production of a cheque guarantee card) but is at the discretion of one of its credit officers, who will conduct an assessment while the customer is in the store. If an application is approved, the card can be granted on the spot.

GEC

GEC – GE Capital, part of General Electric Corporation of America – issues cards on behalf of individual store chains, currently Burton Group and House of Fraser.

The Burton Group – which includes Debenhams, Burtons, Top Shop, Principles, Dorothy Perkins, Evans, and Champion Sport – has around 3 million cards issued.

House of Fraser – which includes Army & Navy, Barkers, DH Evans, Dickins & Jones, Harrods, and Rackhams – has around 1 million cards issued.

There is a significant difference between a GE card and one, say, issued by M&S. With the M&S card, it is the store chain itself which operates and finances the card. It, therefore, sets its own issuing criteria and takes the risk for fraud and credit losses. Where a store uses a GE card, however, it is GE which sets the criteria for granting a card and which bears the risks. In practice, GE may delegate responsibility for issuing cards to the individual stores, but the stores will be applying credit scoring criteria (see Chapter Six) as set down by GE. The lack of financial risk for the store is one major attraction of using a third-party like GE, rather than operating its own card. It also avoids placing financial pressure on the balance sheet of store groups.

GE Capital also runs a Private Label operation, which provides credit arrangements for retail stores to offer to their customers. These arrangements are used by the likes of Dixons, Bentalls, Tandy, Currys and Kwik Fit. In the main, this operation functions without the issue of an actual credit card – credit is extended for a limited period of time for a particular range of products – although Private Label does issue one store card, for Laura Ashley.

Fuel Cards

Fuel cards are exactly what the name implies. They are payment cards which can – with very few exceptions – be used simply to pay for fuel. They are generally issued by companies to their employees as a means of avoiding the misuse that could accompany the provision of more traditional credit cards – that is, employees using them to pay for a range of other goods and letting the company pay the bill. The UK fuel card market is almost entirely dominated by the heavy goods business, although there is also a significant fleet business. Cards are not normally issued to the private motorist. Fuel card issuers will provide companies using their cards with very detailed breakdown figures of purchases by employees, thus keeping the scope for abuse to a minimum.

The market leader in fuel cards is PHH Vehicle Management Services Limited, which has 380,000 cards in issue. PHH brands are Allstar (aimed at company car fleets), Allstar Diesel Direct and Allstar DERV. The two latter cards account for 20,000 of the total issued, with the remaining 360,000 being Allstar cards.

The second biggest player is the Harpur Group, with its Overdrive and Dialcard cards. It also provides a third-party processing service and administers the ESSO card.

The biggest oil company in this field is BP, with a card base of 100,000. Its brand names include BP Supercharge, BP Plus Bunker Card, BP Agency Card and BP Plus Europa. Interestingly, BP uses PHH to process its card operations.

FOUR

THE UNITED KINGDOM MARKET: STATISTICS

Market Penetration

The UK adult population is 45.2m of which 51.8% is female. Some 28.2m form part of the working population of which 26m are actually employed. There are 22.6m households in the UK.

Table 1 on page 40 shows the consumer profiles and card penetration of credit and charge cards in 1991.

Around 33% of the adult population hold a credit card and some 26% of credit cardholders have two or more cards. Proportionately more males than females hold credit cards. The holdings are biased towards the ABC1 (professional, managerial and clerical) socio-economic groups. Nationally some 31% of the population is classified as DE (state pensioners and casual workers) socio-economic groups, and yet only 18% of credit cardholders fall into these groups.

Similarly some 32% of the population is aged 55 years or over and yet only 25% of credit cardholders are aged 55 years or over. 8% of credit cardholders are under the age of 25 years while 17.5% of the population is in the 15-24 age group. However, it should be remembered that no person under the age of 18 years can normally hold a credit card.

There is a strong regional bias to cardholders living in London and the South East of England.

Table 1: Credit/Charge Cards:
Consumer Profiles and Card Penetration, 1991

	Customer Profile	Card Penetration	
	All Credit Cards	One Card	Two or More Cards
Number of Credit/Charge cardholders	**(14.3m)**	**(74%)**	**(26%)**
Sex			
Male	53	68	32
Female	47	82	18
Social Class			
AB	32	65	35
C1	33	74	26
C2	23	82	18
DE	13	86	14
Age			
18–20	2	86	14
21–24	6	79	21
25–34	22	73	27
35–44	27	71	29
45–54	20	72	28
55–64	13	76	24
65+	12	83	17
Region			
South East	41	69	31
South West	8	77	23
Midlands/Wales	23	77	23
North	21	77	23
Scotland	7	79	21

Plastic cards in issue

There are more bank-issued credit cards in issue than there are any other type of credit or charge cards. However, as **Table 2** on page 41 shows, the numbers of credit cards peaked in 1990. After the introduction of annual fees in 1990 and 1991, many people who had more than one card were only prepared to pay one set of fees and so divested themselves of their other cards.

Table 2: Plastic Cards in Issue, UK, 1985–1993								
Cards (000) 1985	1986	1987	1988	1989	1990	1991	1992	1993
Credit cards 19,595	21,967	24,526	25,872	28,563	30,026	27,095	28,020	28,000
Charge cards 1,749	1,873	1,997	2,156	2,849	3,309	3,440	3,600	3,800
Store cards 8,700	9,800	11,000	11,800	12,600	13,300	13,500	13,650	13,700
Debit cards nil	nil	nil	N/A	13,589	18,952	21,779	22,566	24,188
Total 30,044	33,640	37,523	39,828	57,601	65,587	65,814	67,836	69,688

Another interesting feature is the rise of debit cards. The growth in debit cards was, in part, fuelled by the introduction of annual fees for credit cards. Again, many of those customers who did not take extended credit on their credit cards switched to debit cards rather than pay a fee.

The figures show that the introduction of fees in 1990-91 led to a reduction in credit cards in issue, while there was also a similar size increase in the number of debit cards during this period. However, debit cards were a new and growing market at this time, anyway. Table 2 also indicates that store cards constitute a substantial part of the payment card market in terms of cards in issue although Table 3 indicates that they are relatively insignificant in terms of usage.

Turnover by type of card

Table 3 shows that the average turnover on charge cards is far higher than that for credit cards and debit cards. This indicates that charge cardholders tend to be from a higher income group and have a higher propensity to spend. This table also shows a steady increase in debit card use since they were introduced in 1988-89, as people become more familiar with them and the number of outlets accepting debit cards increases.

Table 3: Average Turnover by Type of Card, 1985–1993								
Turnover/ card £ 1985	1986	1987	1988	1989	1990	1991	1992	1993
Charge cards 1,687	1,879	2,157	2,552	2,793	3,373	2,821	2,957	3,045
Credit cards 536	601	679	793	832	930	1,095	1,174	1,316
Debit cards nil	nil	nil	nil	124	271	445	581	741
Store cards 119	133	150	172	190	212	223	234	241

Table 4 shows that credit and store cards have a higher average transaction value than the charge or debit card. The reason for this is that these cards tend to be used for buying big consumer and household items, rather than for paying for, say, clothing or restaurant bills. It is interesting to note that the average transaction value for debit cards continues to increase, while the credit card remained static in 1993.

Table 4: Average Transaction by Type of Card, 1985–1993

Transaction Value £	1985	1986	1987	1988	1989	1990	1991	1992	1993
Charge cards	25.03	26.59	28.74	30.92	31.81	34.57	26.55	26.22	27.00
Credit cards	27.07	29.23	31.83	34.24	36.58	39.97	42.48	45.38	45.38
Debit cards	nil	nil	nil	nil	24.85	26.61	26.88	25.19	27.11
Store cards	31.48	34.39	37.43	40.60	43.44	47.01	50.17	51.61	53.15

VISA and MasterCard Credit/Charge Cards

Table 5 shows the number of VISA and MasterCard credit and charge cards in issue.

Table 5: Credit Cards in Issue in the UK, 1985–1993

Cards (000)	1985	1986	1987	1988	1989	1990	1991	1992	1993
MasterCard	8,515	9,846	11,370	11,454	11,839	11,876	11,104	9,879	9,947
VISA	11,080	12,121	13,156	14,418	16,724	18,150	15,991	15,773	15,271
Total	19,595	21,967	24,526	25,872	28,563	30,026	27,095	25,652	25,218

There are more VISA cards issued than MasterCards. MasterCard has shown very little increase since 1988, whereas VISA has been growing quite steadily until 1992 but reflects development of debit cards. The reason for the difference in growth patterns is that VISA has operated under an open membership policy and so more and more banks and building societies have been able to join and so more VISA cards have been issued. MasterCard operated a closed membership policy in the UK until the mid-1980s and hence has fewer members and cardholders. There are inconsistencies in the number of cards in issue between Table 5 and Table 6, caused, it is believed, by differing bases of recording the data. However the trends are similar.

The turnover on both VISA and MasterCards continues to grow – and always at a higher rate than inflation (see Table 6 on page 43). However, as the table shows, the credit card market has not escaped the impact of the recession.

Table 6 MASTERCARD AND VISA 1983–1993

End–December	1983	1984	1985	1986	1987	1988	1989	1990	1991	1992	1993
MASTERCARD											
Credit Outstanding (£ millions) (a)	1,258	1,504	1,901	2,346	2,869	3.003	3,191	3,679	3,840	3,827	3,793
Number of Cards in Issue (thousands) (b)	6,823	7,589	8,515	9,846	11,370	11,454(a)	12,128	12,294	11,554	11,169	10,351
Number of Accounts (thousands) (c)	5,529	6,133	6,923	8,067	9,409	9,829 (a)	10,428	10,098	9,056	9,177	8,926
During the year:											
Value of Turnover (£ millions)	3,153	3,955	5,032	6,287	8,156	9,418	10,816	11,970	12,686	13,024	13,790
VISA											
Credit Outstanding (£ millions)	1,335	1,694	2,146	2,539	2,907	3,342	3,733	4,537	4,823	5,075	5,371
Number of Cards in issue (thousands)(b)	8,994	9,942	11,080	12,121	13,106	14,318	16,485	17,552	15,257	15,307	15,119
Number of Accounts (thousands) (c)	7,465	8,191	9,240	9,948	10,779	11,776	13,703	14,409	12,239	12,060	11,904
During the year:											
Value of Turnover (£ millions)	3,244	4,088	5,472	6,927	8,457	11,026	12,996	15,772	16,664	18,248	19,718
MASTERCARD AND VISA											
Percentage of balances incurring interest	70%	70%	69%	67%	64%	62%	62%	59%	66%	67%	69%

(a) Due to a change in the reporting basis, the figures for 1988 onwards are not consistent with those for previous years.
(b) Excludes cards issued by building societies
(c) Excludes accounts operated by building societies.

Source: BBA Annual Abstract of Banking Statistics.

For MasterCard, there has been a reduction in outstanding balances each year since 1991. With VISA, the trend has been upwards, but this is at least in part because an increasing number of VISA cards have been issued.

VISA outstanding balances continue to grow albeit at a slower rate than in the 1980s. The percentage of balances incurring interest was at around 70 per cent during the early 1980s, before falling back to nearer 60 per cent at the end of the 1980s, early 1990s. This proportion is now rising again. It is perhaps the most crucial figure as far as the card issuer's profitability is concerned.

Of course, if it gets it wrong, it can take the card operation from profit to loss.

Charge Cards in Issue

As **Table 7** shows, in the past three to four years, the charge card market continues to grow in absolute terms. Amex, however, remains the market leader although it had the same number of cards in 1993 as in 1988. VISA is making good progress aided by the Co-operative Bank's 'free-for-life' VISA gold card programme.

Table 7: Charge Cards in Issue, 1985–1993									
Cards (000)	**1985**	**1986**	**1987**	**1988**	**1989**	**1990**	**1991**	**1992**	**1993**
Amex	836	951	1,006	1,100	1,200	1,300	1,300	1,100	1,100
Diners Club	315	282	289	278	300	300	300	300	300
MasterCard									
Gold	nil	nil	nil	nil	289	418	450	475	500
VISA Gold	nil	nil	nil	nil	161	232	585	797	906
Other	598	640	702	778	899	1,059	1,140	1,200	1,200
Total	1,749	1,873	1,997	2,156	2,849	3,309	3,775	3,872	4,006

Overall, Amex and Diners are accepted at around only a third of the number of outlets which accept credit cards. **Table 8** on page 45 shows that there was a fall in the number of outlets taking charge cards during 1990. This was due to a revolt on the part of merchants, who objected to what they saw as the excessive merchant service fee charged by Amex and Diners by refusing to accept their cards. At this stage, the two companies were asking around 4-5 per cent of the value of each transaction; a figure which is now down to around 3-4 per cent. In 1994, Amex state that some 180,000 outlets accept their cards in the UK.

Table 8: Charge Card Outlets, 1981–1993								
Outlets (000)	1981	1985	1987	1989	1990	1991	1992	1993
Total	84	201	258	279	265	290	N/A	N/A
Year on year growth		24.4%	13.3%	4.0%	-5.0%	9.4%	N/A	N/A

The number of outlets accepting VISA and MasterCard continue to grow as shown in **Table 9**.

Table 9: VISA & MasterCard Outlets, UK, 1981–1993								
Outlets (000)	1981	1985	1987	1989	1990	1991	1992	1993
Total	352	471	571	753	815	868	904	948
Year on year growth		7.6%	10.1%	14.8%	8.2%	6.5%	4.1%	4.9%

Store cards

There around 13.6 million store cards in issue (see Table 2 on page 41). The numbers have remained static over the past four to five years: This is partly due to the recession. It is also because, where store cards finance their own cards (see Chapter Three), they can find their balance sheets coming under pressure. For this reason, many of them haven't sought to expand their card customer base as they did in the 1980s. Others have responded by bringing in an outside provider of finance, like GEC, (see Chapter Three) to finance their store card operations.

Compared with VISA and MasterCard, the turnover figures for store cards are relatively low; store cards account for around 10 per cent of the total expenditure on payment cards as shown in **Table 10**. The rate of growth of store card transactions is slowing down, which also reflects the impact of the recession and the consequential change in consumer payment habits.

Table 10: Store Cards, Value of Transaction, 1985–1993								
Store cards	1985	1986	1987	1988	1989	1990	1991	1992	1993
Transactions (£m)	1,039	1,307	1,647	2,030	2,389	2,821	3,010	3,200e	N/A
% Growth	16.3%	25.8%	26.0%	23.3%	17.7%	18.1%	6.7%	6.3%	N/A

Debit cards

Table 11 shows the number of debit cards in issue in the UK

There are two: VISA Delta and Switch. NatWest bank is a Switch issuer and it also places on its Switch cards, the MasterCard Maestro brand to give its Switch cards an international capability. Maestro is the international debit brand of MasterCard.

VISA Delta is an international brand although in practice, Delta is used in the UK whilst retaining VISA as the international element of the brand.

One reason why so many Switch cards are in issue is that the banks simply added the Switch logo to their cheque guarantee cards.

Table 11: Debit Cards in Issue, 1989–1993					
Debit cards (000)	**1989**	**1990**	**1991**	**1992**	**1993**
VISA Delta	4,430	7,540	8,310	10,219	11,187
Switch	9,159	11,412	11,804	12,377	12,930
Total	13,589	18,952	20,114	22,596	24,117

Market Shares and Volume of Transactions

Table 12, below, shows that Switch has the greater market share but VISA has the greater number of transactions. This indicates that Switch transactions tend to be of higher value than VISA ones.

In the future, we are likely to see a faster rate of growth with debit cards than with credit cards. Indeed, in 1990, an industry leader commented that the battle for the credit card is over but the battle for the debit card is yet to begin. Subsequent years have shown this observation to be correct. The market for credit cards is more or less saturated; however, there is plenty of scope for the continued growth of debit cards.

Table 12: Volume of Debit Card Transactions, 1989–1993					
Transactions (m)	**1989**	**1990**	**1991**	**1992**	**1993**
VISA Delta	52	121	190	253	315
Switch	16	71	169	269	344
Total	68	192	359	522	659

Table 13 on page 47 shows the membership of Switch. The card issuing associates all issue through arrangements with the Midland Bank. NatWest is a dominant issuer of Switch cards.

Table 13: Membership Structure of the Switch Consortium, 1993		
Issuing and Acquiring Members	Bank of Scotland Cyldesdale Bank Midland Bank National Westminster Bank Royal Bank of Scotland	
Issuing Members	Halifax BS Lloyds Bank	
Acquiring Members	Barclays Bank Lloyds Bank	
Card Issuing Associates *Source: Switch*	Allied Irish Banks (GB) Bank of Ireland (GB) Britannia BS Chelsea BS Cumberland BS Derbyshire BS	Norwich & Peterborough BS Southdown BS Whiteway Laidler Bank Yorkshire BS

Table 14 shows the membership structure of Delta.

Table 14: Membership Structure of Delta

The following are VISA Delta issuers:
    Abbey National
    First Trust Bank
    Barclays Bank
    Co-operative Bank
    Girbobank (part of Alliance & Leicester)
    Lloyds Bank
    Nationwide Building Society
    TSB

FIVE

THE MARKETING OF
PAYMENT CARDS

There are two broad target groups in the marketing of payment cards: the card
acceptors, the merchants; and the cardholders, the users.

Card Acceptors

Payment cards are marketed to the card acceptors on the basis of the advantages
they will supposedly bring to the merchant. We have already looked at these in
Chapter Two, however, briefly, they are:

- **Increased sales.** The card issuers argue that accepting payment cards will
  boost the merchant's level of sales. While this argument may have held
  sway when relatively few outlets accepted payment cards, now that
  almost every shop on the high street will do so, it is likely to be less of a
  factor. The reverse is probably true: if a merchant doesn't accept payment
  by plastic, it is likely to lose sales. It needs to accept them to maintain,
  rather than increase, its position.

- **Security.** Whereas cash can be stolen, a credit card voucher is of little
  value to a thief.

- **Cheaper than cash.** It is estimated that the cost of handling cash –
  because of the security needed – can be up to 12-14 per cent of the total
  cost of a transaction, although the average cost is probably around 3-5 per
  cent, depending on the amount handled.

- **Guaranteed payment.** Provided a merchant has followed all the acceptance
  rules laid down by the card issuer, payment is guaranteed. There is no
  need to worry about fraud or credit risks.

- **Same day value.** Most payment card transactions are treated as cleared
  funds on the day they are deposited – unlike cheques which can take three

days or more to clear. However, this is not true of the charge cards Amex and Diners which can take several days to clear. Because these organisations do not have branch networks, the card acceptor has to send the vouchers by post, and then wait for payment to be made either by cheque or direct credit to the bank. Recently, one of the high street banks switched to this method for non-automated transactions.

History of the relationship between issuers and retailers

The relationship between the issuing banks and their target retailer market has undergone a number of transformations since credit cards were first launched in the UK.

Barclays was the first bank in this country to enter the market, with the launch of Barclaycard in 1966. At this time, it acted as both the card-issuing bank and the merchant-acquiring bank, as it signed up retailers to accept its card directly.

Then in 1972, Access was formed by Lloyds, Midland, National Westminster and The Royal Bank of Scotland. The Access banks formed the Joint Credit Card Company, with the task of signing up merchants to accept Access cards. For a number of years there were just two merchant acquirers: Barclays for VISA; and the Joint Credit Card Company for Access.

This situation continued until 1987, when the market was faced with a number of changes. The credit card industry was referred to the Monopolies and Mergers Commission; and the banks themselves began to realise the importance of having a direct relationship with the retailers – rather than going through a third party.

That same year, Lloyds broke ranks and applied to become a member of VISA, which lead to it issuing a VISA debit card in 1988. In 1989, Lloyds formed its own merchant acquisition business in the shape of CardNet. CardNet began signing merchants to accept both MasterCard and VISA.

Once Lloyds had gone down the dual route, it prompted a scramble among the other banks to start signing merchants directly. Barclays and Bank of Scotland joined MasterCard and set about signing merchants; Midland and NatWest also went dual by joining VISA and began acquiring merchants.

Midland, NatWest, Clydesdale, Royal Bank and Bank of Scotland went on to set up the Switch system to operate debit cards. In this way, they could offer merchants a triple package to merchants: Switch, VISA and MasterCard. This move was later followed by Barclays and Lloyds, who also became merchant acquiring members of Switch.

The shake up in the payment card market and the ensuing competition it generated led to a price war among the banks. The average merchant-service charge levied by the banks fell from 2.2 per cent in 1987 to 1.6 per cent in 1994. However, with everyone cutting rates, the banks found they needed to compete on grounds other than just price. As a result, the banks have tried to lock in their larger retailers by developing bespoke services for them. For example, where the merchant has sophisticated electronic point-of-sale equipment, the bank will do its best to integrate its services with that system to minimise the amount of paper involved in transactions.

Despite the banks' best efforts to entice the retailers, there is a history of animosity between the two sides. The retailers have tended to baulk at paying what they see as the excessive charges levied by the banks for accepting payment cards, and have used their buying muscle to force down the rates they have to pay.

The retailers argued that it was unreasonable for the banks to charge, say, 1.6 per cent of the value of goods paid for with a credit card, compared with just 10p for purchases by cheque. For example, on goods costing £50, the merchant service charge would be around £0.80 – 70p more than if the same goods were paid for by cheque.

This problem has largely been created by the banks themselves who got their pricing wrong when they introduced cheque guarantee cards providing guaranteed payments to retailers without an appropriate charge. They have consistently charged unrealistically low prices for handling cheques to which, of course, the retailers have become accustomed. This means that when the banks have tried to charge a more representative rate for payment card transactions, these appear to be overpriced by comparison.

The banks' problems in this area were compounded in 1987, when Barclays introduced its VISA Connect debit card. Barclays tried to levy a credit-card-style merchant service charge for Connect, where the merchant would pay a percentage of the value of each transaction. This was prompted partly by the desire to impose a level of charging which reflected the cost to the bank, and partly because of the philosophy that *a VISA card is a VISA card is a VISA card,* and whether credit or debit, should be treated identically.

However, the retailers remained unimpressed and firmly opposed such a move. They made it clear they would refuse to accept Connect cards unless, for payment purposes, they were treated like cheques and subject to a flat-rate fee for each transaction.

The retailers' purchasing power would have put them in a fairly powerful negotiating position in any event, but in this case, they were aided by the pricing tactics of Connect's rival debit card, Switch, which seemed happy to operate on a per-transaction basis. After a series of public rows, Barclays capitulated. It agreed to operate the cards on the basis of charging around 10-12p for each transaction, that is, broadly comparable to what the retailers were used to paying for cheques.

51

VISA now has one interchange fee for credit cards based on a percentage of the sales value and a separate fee for debit cards. This is a fee per transaction, thereby reflecting merchant resistance to being charged as a percentage of the value of the transaction.

Cardholders

On the other side of the marketing equation from the card acceptors are the cardholders.

The basic aims behind a credit card issuer's marketing philosophy are threefold. It wants to encourage people to take up its cards; it wants the cards to be used regularly; and it wants as high a proportion of customers as possible to take extended credit. For these reasons, some companies will try to discourage dormant accounts and have taken steps to deter customers who are not taking credit.

The initial stage for any card issuer is, of course, to reach the potential customers in the first place. The way in which the card issuer targets potential cardholders will depend on what distribution channels it has available.

- **Branch networks.** The banks and other organisations with large branch networks will tend to use these outlets to promote their cards. Branches will often be given sales targets and required to identify and approach likely candidates from their customers. The advantage of this method is that it is a fairly low-cost means of distributing cards.

  Historically, however, there have been disadvantages for the issuing bank in this approach. In the early 1970s, some branch managers would grant credit cards to customers who had already exceeded their loan or overdraft facilities, on the basis that they took a cash advance with which to pay off the existing debt. The effect of this would be that the manager was relieved of a problem but the debt had simply been transferred from the banking operation to the credit card operation – and the bank overall was no better, and, indeed, probably worse off.

  Organisations which do not have a branch network, or only a very limited number of branches have to rely more heavily on a battery of other tactics. These include: advertising, public relations, direct mail, and personal recommendations.

- **Advertising.** This is by far the most expensive route to go. In general, advertising is used to create a level of awareness of the product, rather than to drum up additional members directly. If it is used to recruit new cardholders, it can be immensely expensive. In Save & Prosper's experience, you can spend £50-£75 on advertising for each new account generated as a result. This assumes advertising is not supported by other marketing activities. If an advertising campaign is to be successful at obtaining new customers, it usually has to be run in conjunction with another marketing element, such as direct mail or public relations.

- **Direct response advertising.** Direct response, or coupon advertising, is where readers are invited to either telephone or send in for further information about a product. Save & Prosper aims to spend around £10 for each individual who contacts the company in each inquiry. However, as around 40 per cent of these will go on to open accounts, this works out to around £25 for each new customer. Many other organisations operating credit cards are prepared to spend double that figure or even more. These organisations are working on the basis that it will be three or four years before they move into profit on the new accounts – whereas Save & Prosper would expect to start making money on new payment card customers after a year or two.

- **Public relations.** As has been stated, using advertising alone can be very expensive. However, it can be made more cost effective if a campaign coincides with favourable press comment. In Save & Prosper's experience, an accolade by an independent journalist can increase the public's response to advertising threefold. While positive public relations can make this kind of difference, it is important to remember that there is a limit to how much of it a company can generate. The media will only recommend your product if it really is better than those of the opposition.

- **Direct mail.** Like advertising, direct mail can be an expensive business. Although it can be more finely directed than general newspaper advertising, in Save & Prosper's experience, it translates into only a 1 per cent response rate. Whereas, as we have said, if individuals contact us in response to a newspaper advertisement, the conversion rate to customers is some 40 per cent.

- **Personal recommendation.** If a recommendation by a journalist in a newspaper can drum up business, so can a recommendation from a friend or colleague. Personal recommendations are an important marketing channel and many payment card companies, including Save & Prosper, will offer incentives to encourage existing customers to introduce new people.

Getting a card issued is, however, only half of the battle. Once a new customer has joined, the card issuer then has to persuade him or her to actually use it. There are three main methods for doing this: education, competitions and sales promotions.

- **Education.** When someone gets a payment card for the first time, he or she may not know where to use or even, quite literally, how to use it. This lack of knowledge creates a barrier to use which the issuer needs to help overcome. Companies will attempt to do this by providing information which takes new customers through the process step by step.

  Once a customer has learned to use the card, the issuer then wants to encourage him or her to use it more and more. That particular card may be in competition with all the other cards which the customer holds – and so the issuer wants to ensure that its card is the one that comes out of the wallet whenever a purchase is being made. To try to do this, the company may run use initiatives like competitions or sales promotions.

- **Competitions.** Customers can qualify, by using their cards, for entry into competitions where the prize may be a holiday, a car, or even a trip on Concorde.

- **Sales promotions.** These would include schemes like Air Miles, where customers can qualify for free air travel, and Profile Points, a scheme run by Barclays where points are accumulated each time the card is used and can then be swopped for goods from a catalogue. These schemes are rather like alcoholism; it is easy to get addicted and usage steadily increases.

Dormant accounts cost the issuing companies money. Even if a card is not being used, the company still needs to have the funds available to cover the credit it offers, and the issuer is still exposed to the risk of fraud. For this reason, some companies run promotions aimed specifically at those accounts which have not been used for some time. If an account is dormant, when it comes up for renewal, instead of issuing a new card automatically, a company may write to ask whether the card is still wanted. Sometimes it will operate on the basis that unless the customer responds saying he or she does still want the card, it will be assumed that it is no longer needed.

But it is important to realise that the companies do not just want customers to use their cards, they want them to take extended credit, as that is where the issuers make their profits.

Customers who never take credit are known as "free riders", because they do not actually pay anything for the service they receive. However, with the introduction of annual fees on many cards, the term "free rider" is becoming a little dated. The only other source of income for the issuers is the merchant service charge paid by the merchant, so card issuers may not generate adequate profits. This is not always the case, however. When interest rates are low the income from the merchant service charge will normally be greater than the cost of financing the transactions made by the cardholder, so a card issuer will still make some income from its free riders. But when interest rates go up, the story may be different: a company may actually be losing money on those who never take extended credit. It was for this reason that, in 1990-91, some payment card companies began introducing annual fees.

Some 40-50 per cent of credit card customers are taking extended credit at any one time – and they account on average for around 65 per cent of the total credit outstanding. Free riders, therefore, will tend to owe less on their credit cards. The proportion of free riders an individual company has can have a significant effect on its income, and so impact on the interest rate and the other charges it imposes.

Save & Prosper, for example, specifically targets its marketing at those who will take extended credit. The result of this is that a higher proportion of its customers will pay interest on the outstanding balances on their card at any one time. Because so many customers are paying interest on their outstanding balances, Save & Prosper can afford to charge a lower rate of interest than many of its competitors.

Interestingly, however, research by Save & Prosper suggests that people do not shop around for the most competitive interest rate. Credit cardholders may complain about the levels they are charged, but very few, it seems, will do anything about it. Of the 16 million adults holding credit cards in this country; 40-50 per cent will be taking extended credit at any one time. Of these 7-9 million people, research suggests only 2-3 per cent will actually change in order to find a better deal from another issuer.

This fact has important implications for the card issuers. Quite simply, there is very little point in cutting interest rates (and consequently earnings) if customers are not price sensitive. You will not create more business as a result, but you will reduce your income.

Some groups of cardholders are, however, very sensitive to other charges. When card issuers introduced annual fees, it proved an extremely effective way of shaking out many of the free riders among their customers.

On average, credit card customers will borrow around 40 per cent of their credit limit – almost regardless of what that limit may be. One tactic, therefore, for boosting card use is simply to up the limit by, say, 10 per cent. Within six to nine months, a card issuer is likely to see a consequential increase in that customer's borrowing. This phenomena was particularly noticeable during the 1970s and 1980s when banks granted across-the-board, automatic credit limit increases to their better clients.

History of the relationship between card issuers and cardholders

When Barclaycard was launched in 1966, many in the banking industry did not believe that the scheme would take off. They were nearly right. Barclaycard's progress was slow until it was boosted in 1972 by the arrival of the rival credit card Access.

The Access banks launched their product with a major television and press campaign and an unsolicited mailshot of the card to prospective users. The effect of the campaign was dramatic. Almost overnight, there were three million cards in circulation and the profile of credit cards in general had been raised significantly.

Such saturation marketing was not without its difficulties, however. Many commentators were outraged that people were apparently wantonly being encouraged to get into debt; and there were numerous reports of inappropriate credit limits being set – with bosses getting lower limits than their secretaries. One result of the outcry, was a clause in the Consumer Credit Act 1974 which explicitly forbade any company sending out unsolicited cards.

Nevertheless, with the arrival of Access, credit cards had been put firmly on the map – and Barclaycard began to take off.

This phenomena of one company benefiting from publicity about a rival is continuing on a smaller scale even today. When Save & Prosper launched its credit card in 1987, the ensuing publicity translated into many applications for the card. Some six months later, however, the numbers coming in were beginning to fall away, until Chase Manhattan launched its own card. When this happened, many journalists covering the launch also mentioned Save & Prosper's earlier initiative, and applications began to pick up again as a result.

The overall market for credit cards in the UK is probably at around saturation point. But while there may be no more room for growth in overall numbers of cards issued, there is still plenty of scope for individual issuers to expand their market share at the expense of their competitors. As we have seen in the previous chapter, however, there is still considerable potential for growth in the number of debit cards in issue.

Co-branding and affinity cards

Co-branding and affinity cards (see Chapter Three) have been introduced by the issuers as a means of targeting people they otherwise might not reach. The card issuer gets the benefit of access to the third party's membership list or marketing information, and the third party also benefits from the arrangement (see below). However, as the card is stamped with the name of the affinity group or co-brandee, the arrangement may be at the expense of the card issuer's own brand awareness.

With co-branded cards like those operated by both Ford and General Motors, the arrangement is simply an alternative way of marketing their products. By using the card, customers will qualify for a discount if they buy a new car from the relevant manufacturer. In this way, the car manufacturer hopes to ensure customer loyalty and so boost sales.

Co-branding is about managing two distinct brand identities which will normally have discreet functional and emotional identities. Co-branding is not about using a single supplier. Although, for example, Rover cars may have Lucas lights and a Honda engine, as far as the Rover car is concerned, these suppliers remain invisible.

There are dilemmas in the management of co-brands. First, it is necessary to ensure that consumers understand the benefits of linking brands. Second, consumers must not perceive the linking of the two well-known brands as illogical and contradictory. Brand values are very important and partners must be sure that there are no contradictions. For example, you would not expect the bankers Coutts & Co to link with Heinz baked beans.

It is vital that the co-branding advertising is not over complicated. One brand must lead, or a new joint brand must be created, as happened with the Ford Barclaycard. However, the bank, which is the co-branding partner of the GM VISA MasterCard remains invisible. The bank in this case is HFC Trust, but it is not publicised.

Co-branding creates many marketing advantages. For example, the Ford Barclaycard brings increased distribution outlets via Ford showrooms; it improves the existing profile points loyalty scheme, it means increased marketing budgets with investment from both Barclaycard and Ford and it provides the means to differentiate a card in the market.

Co-branded cards are not the same as affinity cards as, with true co-branding, both names are visible. Barclaycard Ford is an example of true co-branding, while the GM card is really an example of a supplier of an invisible bank brand.

Leverage of brand power can create enormous benefits, but there is a scarcity of brands where co-branding can be undertaken successfully.

With affinity cards, the organisation involved provides the card issuer with access to its members in return for an income from cards issued as a result. The affinity group members are contacted, ostensibly by the organisation and invited to apply for a card. The card issuer pays a fixed sum, usually around £5, to the institution for each account opened and a percentage of subsequent expenditure on the card, usually around 25p for every £100.

For the cardholder, the attraction is intended to be that he or she provides financial support for the organisation, and also benefits from the status that being a member of such a group conveys. However, the terms and conditions offered with these cards are generally no better, and sometimes worse, than those more widely available.

SIX

CREDIT SCORING AND ASSESSMENT

Credit Assessment

This chapter covers credit assessment in general and has a section on credit scoring which, of course, measures the statistical probability that credit will be satisfactorily repaid.

How to qualify for a loan

Before banks will lend money, there are generally six basic factors they will look at, whether the customer is an individual or a multi-national company.

The six questions are:

- What does the customer want the money for?

- How long does he want to borrow for?

- How much does he want?

- Is this amount enough for his needs?

- How is he planning to repay the money?

- Is there any security available?

A bank will weigh up the answers to these questions before deciding whether or not to go ahead with a loan.

What happens when the "loan" is a credit card?

With credit card lending, exactly the same set of factors as we referred to above are at work.

- What does the customer want the money for? Credit card finance should be short term.

- How long does he want to borrow for? It is revolving credit – see Chapter Two.

- How much does he want? The credit limit must be set at a realistic level – one that the customer can afford to pay back.

- Is this amount enough for his needs? The banks do not want to set the limit too low, or the customer will constantly be exceeding his limit so causing them operational problems.

- How is he planning to repay the money? Out of current income, at a minimum of 5 per cent a month?

- Is there any security available? Credit cards are generally unsecured (although there is no reason why banks could not ask for security in appropriate cases – as some do in the US).

Assessing risk

Again, whatever the size or type of loan, and whoever the customer, the bank will want to determine whether or not he is a good risk. The credit provider looks at stability, ability to repay, credit experience and past credit performance. A strong showing in one area can compensate for another area. For example an individual who has just taken a new job in another part of the country may show instability but is a good risk as a result of income and occupation.

Stability

The key to creditworthiness is stability. Banking experience shows that if a customer is settled in his house, his work and in his relationship with his bank, and in other aspects of his life (see below), he is likely to be a better credit risk.

Generally speaking, banks will look for a customer who has owned his own home, has been with his current employer, and with his current bankers for a specific period of time. However, these rules do not need to be applied completely rigidly. Just because a customer does not meet one of these criteria does not mean he would be automatically rejected. It would just be one of the factors taken into consideration before deciding whether or not to grant a loan. If there is instability, however, an application will tend to be scrutinised far more closely.

Marital status is another factor which is strongly linked to stability. Divorced people will very often inevitably have greater demands put on their income. They may be supporting second mortgages, meeting large maintenance payments (or relying on maintenance payments which are delayed or do not materialise) – or just living more haphazard lifestyles because of the turmoil that marriage breakdown can bring in its wake.

Age is another factor which influences the bank's view of stability. Some banks will be reluctant to take on elderly people because of the difficulties of recovering outstanding money if they should die. On the other hand, people in middle age may be deemed to be more settled, living more predictable lives, and so a better risk. The young – those under 25 – are also likely to be considered a greater risk because they will tend to be less experienced in financial matters.

Experience suggests that customers in households which do not have a telephone may also be a poorer risk. Again, this is linked with the question of stability: established households will tend to have a telephone installed. However, the existence of a telephone is becoming less of a factor in determining stability.

Ability to Pay

A bank will want to be sure that a customer has the financial resources for him to service his debt. This would involve looking at his income, whether it be from salary, bonuses, commission, self-employment, or pension. Banks are generally reluctant to take into account any income which is not guaranteed. They would, therefore, be likely to want to discount bonuses and commission. If a client is self-employed, a bank would normally want to see three years certified accounts. This is simply because a high proportion of people who set up in business for themselves go under in their early years.

As well as a person's income, the bank will also look at his outgoings and other commitments. This would include his mortgage, other credit card borrowings, hire purchase, personal loans, and so on. As a general rule of thumb, at Save & Prosper, if someone's debts represent more than 50 per cent of his net income, he would be seen to be already over committed, and, therefore, deemed to be a poor risk. As ever, there are exceptions to this. A person on average earnings of say £20,000 in this position, would be likely to be rejected for being over stretched. However, for someone on, say, £200,000, it might be decided that, although he already had large debts, the remaining income was still large enough to cope with further borrowings.

Card issuers are less concerned with someone's employment category, in terms of whether they are, say, ABC1s, and more interested in the type of business in which they are employed. Indeed, some customers in the higher employment groups may be deemed to be bad risks because they work in sectors which are in decline.

The areas which invite caution will tend to change with the state of the wider economy. In the early 1980s, for example, banks might have been reluctant to lend to people employed in, say, shipbuilding or the steel industry, which were in decline with many people facing redundancy. Whereas in the 1990s, bankers are being looked at very carefully. After the stockmarket crash in 1987, people employed in the securities industry, who might previously have expected to have no problems securing credit, began to be seen as potentially bad risks.

Credit Experience

Such factors as the existing ownership of credit cards, past loans and the existence of a current account or deposit relationship as well as the length of these relationships are very important.

Credit providers are normally more willing to lend to customers with whom they have an existing good relationship.

Past Credit Performance

Banks will generally run a credit check on a customer to find to whether he has a history of defaulting. If the check shows up a County Court Judgment against him, this will obviously be a strongly negative factor. However, it may not necessarily rule him out altogether. If the customer explains the circumstances of the judgment, he was in dispute with a supplier over faulty goods, the bank may still be prepared to accept him.

The Data Protection Act provides customers with their right to ask a credit provider whether or not a credit reference agency has been used and, if so, which agency. The client can then pay a fee of £1 to the agency and obtain a copy of the record held. If it is wrong, the customer can demand that the reference be corrected.

Today, many banks supply what is called "black information" on clients to credit reference agencies. Black information is the term used to describe clients who are either in arrears with their repayments or who are over their credit limits. Normally, if an account is 90 days or more in arrears it will be reported. Banks need to have the clients' permission before releasing this information, but this is usually included in the account rules as a standard condition. Black information serves as a warning to other credit providers that a potential client already has financial difficulties.

A few banks and most finance companies also provide "white information" to credit reference agencies. White information is the details of all lending facilities granted to the client so that a credit provider can build up a picture of a potential customer's credit commitments.

The practice of supplying black information and white information is well established in the USA and provides great benefits to lenders and borrowers alike. Lenders are able to avoid lending money to people who are over extending themselves; and, at least in part, borrowers are prevented from getting themselves into financial difficulties. It is hoped that a similar system will develop in the UK.

Bank References

A bank reference is an opinion provided by the applicant's bank which indicates whether or not the applicant is considered to be a good or bad risk. References are couched in coded language, which only experienced bankers can understand fully. The best reference is "undoubted"; the worst is "we regret we are unable to speak for your figures."

Many card issuers will not bother to take up bank references on potential customers, relying on credit scoring instead (see below). In Save & Prosper's case, we ask customers to supply three months' worth of bank statements. This is usually sufficient to throw up any problems with the account – bounced cheques, non-payment of direct debits, and so on. In fact, looking at a set of statements will often give you a better picture of the state of someone's finances than a bank reference, which may not tell the whole story.

There are other advantages of using statements – some banks now charge for supplying references and the delay often incurred before they are supplied can prolong the entire process. Why make life easy for a competitor?

However, Save & Prosper has encountered some resistance from some customers to supplying statements. It can be seen almost as an invasion of privacy. Customers tend to take the attitude that a decision ought to be able to be made on the basis of the application form, without the need for the supplying of extra information.

The next area to be looked at would be the amount of equity a customer has in his house. Equity in a house is the difference between its current value and that of mortgages (and other loans) secured by the house. For example, if the house is worth £60,000 and the mortgage is £50,000, the equity is the difference, £10,000. Negative equity is where the mortgage and loans exceed the current value of the house, probably because house prices have fallen since it was bought. This means, that if the house were sold, there would be no excess funds available and possibly a debt remaining.

In general, banks prefer to avoid negative equity situations – which could, until the housing market picks up, potentially rule out a large number of people who bought their homes in the late 1980s. The reason for this is that if the customer should default, the bank relies on getting access to the equity in the house to make good what it is owed.

How do all these risk factors tie up with credit scoring?

Credit scoring utilises all the risk factors we have outlined above, and allocates values to each of them. With traditional lending, the bank manager is supposed to weigh up these factors in his mind and made a decision accordingly. With credit scoring, a customer's response to each question is ascribed a score, which is then totalled up to determine whether he has "passed" or "failed", that is, whether he is deemed to be a good or a bad risk.

It is important to remember that a scorecard is intended to 'rank order' risk as opposed to predicting specific levels of risk. That is, it should always be true that a higher score represents a better applicant (lower risk) than a lower score. However, the actual odds of repayment associated with a particular score may in fact change through time as the overall economy gets better or worse.

The advantage credit scoring has over traditional lending is its objectivity. With traditional lending, a bank manager's personal prejudices will inevitably come into play. If he has just been hard hit by, say, an architect who went out of business and defaulted on a loan, with the best will in the world, he is likely to be reluctant to lend immediately to anyone else in that same profession who comes along. However, after a few years, the memory may fade.

The similarities and differences between **judgment** and **credit scoring** are:

Similarities:

- Have same objective

- Evaluate creditworthiness

- Use the same information

- Based on past experience

- Make accept/reject decision

Differences:

- Consistency and objectivity – the same decision will be reached regardless of which lender is used or the "mood" of the lender.

- Use of past experience – whereas judgmental lending relies on the past experience of the individual lender, credit scoring is based on the total experience of the institution.

- Management control – instead of saying "tighten up" or "loosen up" when the economy changes, a manager can make a quantitative change in the cut–off score.

- Productivity – since a scorecard can be implemented to make automatic decisions, or can be used to make the more obvious decisions on both the high and low end.

- Assessment of overall risk – instead of simply making an accept or reject decision, the score predicts the actual odds of becoming good or bad.

The values allocated to each factor in credit scoring are based on empirical research. It is based on an analysis comparing good and bad accounts, and working out what characteristics apply to each. The analysis of what constitutes a 'good' or 'bad' account is usually part of the development process. Using this information, a statistical picture can be build up. This tells the lending organisation that an account which has this set of characteristics has an increased probability of going bad; whereas an account with a different set of characteristics is more likely to be properly run. This information allows banks to build up a score card.

Ideally, credit scoring should be based upon the card issuer's experience. It should be the accounts of your own clients which are being analysed, as this will give a true picture of the characteristics of your particular customer base, rather than being based on the experiences of lending institutions generally.

What usually happens is that a consultant will be employed by a company to study its account records. This analyst will then devise a scoring system, where points are awarded according to the previous experience. This system can be incorporated into a computer programme which automates much of the process. Staff can then simply key in the information, and the computer tells them whether or not a customer is a good or a bad risk. If a customer's score is above a certain level, he gets the loan; if he falls below, the loan is refused.

A typical score card was published in the *Daily Express* and is reproduced on page 66. No bank claimed it as their own but, equally, no bank would wish its score card to be made public. However, this does give a good idea of what a score card looks like.

This brings us on to one of the major disadvantages of credit scoring: its apparent rigidity. Most bank managers would say it misses out a key ingredient, their personal knowledge of the customer. For example, you have a customer who is the chief executive of a large finance house who asks you to issue a credit card to his 18-year-old son. Under credit scoring, the son's application would almost certainly be rejected. However, under traditional lending, as his father's bank manager of many years, you know that, even though you have no formal guarantee from him, if his son were to run into debt, the father's personal pride and reputation would demand that he step in to bail him out. Under the first scenario, you have an important customer feeling disgruntled; under the second, you have an important customer who is satisfied, particularly if he is aware that you treated him as a special case.

Any professional credit scoring consultant would not recommend a credit provider uses the scorecard for all his credit decisions. There should be in place a clear policy on scorecard overrides. For example, those situations which would override the use of a scorecard in the first place – such as underage applicants, as

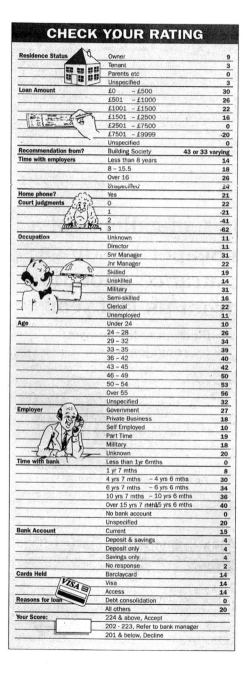

CHECK YOUR RATING

Residence Status	Owner	9
	Tenant	3
	Parents etc	0
	Unspecified	3
Loan Amount	£0 – £500	30
	£501 – £1000	26
	£1001 – £1500	22
	£1501 – £2500	16
	£2501 – £7500	0
	£7501 – £9999	-20
	Unspecified	0
Recommendation from?	Building Society	43 or 33 varying
Time with employers	Less than 8 years	14
	8 – 15.5	18
	Over 16	26
	Unspecified	14
Home phone?	Yes	21
Court judgments	0	22
	1	-21
	2	-41
	3	-62
Occupation	Unknown	11
	Director	11
	Snr Manager	31
	Jnr Manager	22
	Skilled	19
	Unskilled	14
	Military	31
	Semi-skilled	16
	Clerical	22
	Unemployed	11
Age	Under 24	10
	24 – 28	26
	29 – 32	34
	33 – 35	39
	36 – 42	40
	43 – 45	42
	46 – 49	50
	50 – 54	53
	Over 55	56
	Unspecified	32
Employer	Government	27
	Private Business	18
	Self Employed	10
	Part Time	19
	Military	18
	Unknown	20
Time with bank	Less than 1yr 6mths	0
	1 yr 7 mths	8
	4 yrs 7 mths – 4 yrs 6 mths	30
	6 yrs 7 mths – 6 yrs 6 mths	34
	10 yrs 7 mths – 10 yrs 6 mths	36
	Over 15 yrs 7 mths15 yrs 6 mths	40
	No bank account	0
	Unspecified	20
Bank Account	Current	15
	Deposit & savings	4
	Deposit only	4
	Savings only	4
	No response	2
Cards Held	Barclaycard	14
	Visa	14
	Access	14
Reasons for loan	Debt consolidation	0
	All others	20
Your Score:	224 & above, Accept	
	202 - 223, Refer to bank manager	
	201 & below, Decline	

Published in the *Daily Express,* 16 March 1994 and reproduced by kind permission of Express Newspapers.

well as specific reasons for overriding the scorecard whether the initial score is a pass or a fail. These reasons should consist of items for which an insufficient sample existed in the development (eg., if very few people with County Court Judgments were accepted in the past, you cannot know their true performance) as well as when there are other business reasons to override – eg., large deposit relationship with the credit card organisation. The most important thing to avoid is overrides for "gut feelings" which will simply return lending decisions to those made prior to the implementation of the scorecard. In addition, for overrides below the score (where the applicant is accepted anyway), the performance of these accounts should be carefully tracked to ensure they are performing at least as well as those just above the cut–off.

The score can be used with an additional factor (such as disposable income) to determine the appropriate credit limit.

Although credit scoring can take into account whether an individual is an existing customer, it may not give sufficient weight to the customer's previous borrowing experience, notwithstanding the other factors which may, under credit scoring, be regarded as negative If someone has consistently run their account with you in a proper manner, or has a history of borrowing from you and repaying on schedule, this would tend to override many of the other concerns that you might have.

As has been stated, where credit scoring is being used, it should be tailor-made for the credit card organisation. That way, it will take into account any idiosyncrasies of the customer base. However, some credit scoring consultants may offer off-the-peg scoring arrangements. This type of scheme has the advantage that it means credit scoring can be applied straight away, rather than having to wait until you have built up a sufficient account history for analysis.

If a non-personalised score card is used, it is vital that it should be kept constantly under review to reflect your own particular experience. Similarly, if you change your marketing approach and start attracting a different type of customer, you may find that your credit scoring is no longer appropriate, and so needs to be kept under constant review.

Arrangements should also be kept under review to take into account wider economic changes. If a particular sector of the labour market is being hit by a wave of redundancies, you will need to adjust your scoring to reflect this change. It is important to recognise the importance of proper auditing, proper staff training for scorecard users, handling of complaints and reasons for refusal.

Although the scores allocated in each particular category will be set according to statistical analysis, there is some room for discretion at where the card issuer sets its cut off point. Lenders tend to alter the threshold below which credit will not be granted depending on the state of the economy generally. For example, if the maximum achievable score is, say, 1,000 and usually the "pass mark" is 500, a bank may want to lower that figure when times are good to drum up more business (in the knowledge any losses will be offset); and raise it when times are bad. This is done to maximise profits according to the current and projected state of the economy.

It is equally important to monitor if it is a bespoke scorecard. This should include reports that review changes in overall score distribution as well as demographics of your application population. In addition, and even more important, it should include reports that evaluate the validity and effectiveness of the scorecard. Ultimately it is these later reports that demonstrate if and when you would need to replace a scorecard, regardless of whether it is genetic or bespoke.

The Office of Fair Trading and Credit Scoring

In 1983, the Director General of Fair Trading issued a *Guide to Credit Scoring*. This guide acknowledged that credit scoring is an integral part of modern credit assessment and the responsible granting of credit.

The Office of Fair Trading's (OFT) guidance stressed that emphasis should be put on the personal record of the applicant, rather than on non–personal data, such as the district in which the applicant lives.

The OFT mentioned the need to tell applicants why they have been refused credit, but it recognised the need of lenders to protect the integrity of their assessment systems against manipulation and fraud.

The Guide covers the principles of scorecard design, implementation and operation, as well as decision making. It also emphasises the need to establish a complaints procedure, which should be advised to clients.

Fraudulent applications

While credit scoring can be effective at weeding out the financially unstable or incompetent, it is less able to detect those whose applications are simply fraudulent. See Chapter Seven for more details.

The credit limit

The card issuer will set an initial credit limit for each applicant. Generally, it will be between 10–20 per cent of gross income. However, this will vary from issuer to issuer, as well as from cardholder to cardholder – depending on the cardholder's financial situation.

SEVEN

FRAUD AND BAD DEBT

Although fraud and bad debt are rather different issues, with various causes and solutions, we are treating them under the same broad heading because both have cost implications for the card company, and both need to be controlled.

FRAUD

There are several different types of fraud - each of which can be controlled and reduced by a slightly different approach. We will look at the main known types but, as fraudsters are ever inventive, as new safeguards are found, so the cheats are working on new ways to get around them.

Application fraud

This falls into two types: where a fraudster assumes another person's identity for the purposes of his or her application; and financial fraud, where the applicant applies in his own name, but lies about his personal or financial situation.

Assumed identity

With this fraud, an individual impersonates someone else, whose address and bank details he has discovered. He applies for a card using the false name, giving a "new address" and saying that he has just moved. Once the initial information has been obtained, this type of fraud is relatively simply to conduct.

Financial fraud

This is where an individual applies in his own name, but gives fraudulent information about his personal or financial status. He might overstate his income or understate his borrowings and other commitments.

The safeguards against both these types of fraud are to require documentary evidence from applicants to support the information they provide. A card issuer could ask for a mortgage statement, to prove the applicant owns his own home;

wage slips; bank statements, and so on. The card issuer can also do its own checking by telephoning the individual's supposed place of work or his home, to ensure the application is genuine and that he works where he claims to work. However, even this is not foolproof. Fraudsters have been known to forge documents and even use false telephone numbers to deceive card issuers.

Other safeguards which can be implemented at the application stage are examination of the electoral roll and a credit check. A credit check will usually supply details of a person's address, how long he or she has lived there, his date of birth, and, importantly, details of any other credit checks that have been carried out on him. This latter information enables an issuer to tell whether an individual has been applying for numerous other cards. It also shows any County Court Judgments (CCJs) registered against the applicant and so shows a history of defaulting.

Insisting on documentary evidence can largely eliminate the threat of impersonation fraud. It helps reduce, but cannot prevent altogether, the threat of financial fraud.

The application form itself can also be revealing to the trained eye. Some issuers have staff specially trained to scrutinise forms for evidence of fraud. This would include looking for spelling mistakes and crossings out. Both these have been found to sometimes indicate that the supposedly personal information supplied by the applicant is, in fact, unfamiliar because it is false. For example, a form showing the applicant's job as a "Flourist" (rather than "Florist") would set alarm bells ringing.

Intercept Fraud

Intercept fraud is where a card is applied for properly but is then stolen from the postal system before it reaches the applicant.

There are various ways of trying to prevent this - whether by using safer methods of transit, or introducing other safeguards. In areas where levels of intercept fraud are high, an issuer may despatch cards by messenger or by using a private security firm. Alternatively, customers may be asked to collect their new card from a local branch in the case of bank issued cards.

Other safeguards that can be employed include card validation. This is where a card will not be cleared for use (see below) until the rightful recipient has telephoned the bank to say it has arrived safely. The caller will then be asked for personal details, such as date of birth or information relating to his bank account, before the card is cleared for use. Another method is to validate the card when it is used for the first time. When the recipient tries to use the card and the merchant seeks authorisation for its use, the issuer will insist on identifying the cardholder, again, to check his identity.

Card issuers should also be sure to co–operate fully with the investigations branch of the Post Office in its attempts to stamp out mail theft. The Post Office Investigations Branch has a good record of identifying dishonest postal staff.

Lost and Stolen Cards

Wrongful use of lost and stolen cards is the biggest area of credit card fraud. This area is perhaps both the simplest, and the hardest, to tackle. The solution is to persuade credit card customers to take great care of their cards – treating them as cash. However, in practice, customer education is not always easy to achieve.

Apart from persuasion - in leaflets and advertising - credit card companies also impose penalties on customers whose cards fall into the wrong hands. The Consumer Credit Act 1974 allows credit companies to charge cardholders for the first £50 of fraudulent expenditure incurred prior to the theft of the card being reported to the company.

Furthermore, at Save & Prosper, customers may be charged a fee (currently £25) for the re–issue of a lost or stolen card. Another effective technique for bringing the security message home to customers is to write telling them how much the theft of their card has cost the bank.

If cardholders are persistently careless and constantly having cards stolen, the card issuer might decide to close the account.

Fake and Doctored Cards

There are several ways in which fraudsters can tamper with existing cards. They can effectively create their own, by embossing the details of a valid, existing card on to a piece of plastic made up to look like a payment card. The best way of avoiding this type of fraud is to make cards hard to fake. Companies are achieving this by introducing holograms on cards. Where the fraudster attempts to encode the magnetic stripe with valid details, a fraud prevention device, known as its card verification value (CVV), can be used to detect the fraud. Clearly, we are not able to include full details of how the CVV works, for fear of helping potential fraudsters.

Skimming

Skimming is where the information contained in the magnetic stripe on the reverse of the card is copied on to the stripe of another card.

Some companies are experimenting with other methods, such as watermark magnetic stripes where, unless the information comes over in a set format, the authorisation request will be turned down by the card issuer.

Multiple Vouchers

Multiple voucher fraud is conducted by the card acceptor, rather than the card user. In this case, a customer, rightfully, uses his card to pay for goods and services but, instead of producing just one transaction slip, the merchant runs off several. He then forges the customer's signature and banks the vouchers. This type of fraud is usually easy to detect - it is easy to discover who is the merchant. However, if it is a dishonest member of staff who has perpetrated it, he or she may have disappeared by the time it is discovered.

Mail Order

Mail order or "customer not present" transaction fraud is conducted where a fraudster gets hold of a valid card and uses it to order goods and services over the telephone. The simplest way to overcome this is by address checking. The goods will be despatched only to the address registered on the card.

Loss Reduction Methods

Once cards have fallen into the wrong hands, there are several steps card issuers can take to stop them being much use to the fraudster.

Photocards

Photocards are exactly as they sound. The customer's picture appears on the card. This sounds as if it should be a reasonably foolproof method of preventing unauthorised use of the card. However, in practice it may be less so. Several years ago, a senior executive at a credit card company had a card made up in his own name which featured a picture of a gorilla. He was able to use it for four months before he was challenged. Photocards are only as good at preventing fraud as the merchant's staff are at checking that the customer matches the likeness on the card.

It is also thought that photocards will only act as a deterrent while a minority of card issuers are using them. In this instance, they may simply drive fraudsters into targeting other card issuers. If photos appeared on all cards, it is thought the overall amount of fraud would not be reduced.

VISA takes the view that photocards are useful as a marketing tool - people like having their picture on their card - rather than a long-term fraud prevention method. At best, they are seen as a short-term safeguard.

Photocards are also expensive to produce. The cost of putting the customer's picture on the card is roughly equivalent to the cost of the fraud incurred every year on each card in issue (see below).

Integrated Circuit Cards

Integrated Circuit Cards (ICC), or "chip cards" cost around the same to produce as photocards. They are considerably more sophisticated, however. The chip can contain a range of personal information about the cardholder - date of birth and so on - which has to be verified at the point of sale. Chip cards are already being used, apparently successfully, in France but are not yet available in the UK. They are likely to be in wide use by the end of the decade.

Authorisation of Transactions

In the US, all payment card transactions, of whatever value, are authorised automatically. Authorisation is the process whereby the merchant gets the transaction verified as valid by the card issuer; quite simply, the issuer says it is in order for the merchant to go ahead with the transaction. In the UK, however, low-value transactions will not always be authorised and so the opportunity for fraud remains. In the UK, there is a disincentive for all transactions to be checked: not all card acceptors have on-line, point-of-sale, terminals and telephone charges which are higher than in the US, although the cost of calls in the UK is falling.

This situation is changing. In 1992, the Card Payments Group of APACS set up a sub-committee called The Plastic Card Fraud Prevention Forum, (PFPF); to tackle this area. The PFPF brought together people from the UK payment card industry in order to reduce progressively the level below which card transactions are not authorised (their "floor limit"). The floor limit is the amount above which the merchant must obtain authorisation for a transaction. The more transactions which are authorised, the less scope there is for fraud.

User Limits

Card issuers can require that high-value, or other types of transactions (for example, the first one on a new card) must be referred back to them for verification before being authorised. In this instance, the issuer would seek to identify the customer who was attempting to use his card.

There are even systems available which can spot transactions which do not conform to the cardholder's usual spending pattern. When one of these is requested to be authorised, the card issuer can seek proof of identity before authorising the transaction. In due course, the situation may develop where extra proof is required for all transactions.

Merchant Education

As was stated earlier, security devices like photocards are only as good as the merchant's staff are at employing them. Merchant education is an area where there is considerable scope for reducing fraud. Staff need to be trained properly to check photographs, check signatures and to ask for additional proof of identity.

Credit Industry Fraud Avoidance Scheme (CIFAS)

The Credit Industry Fraud Avoidance Scheme (CIFAS) is made up of banks, building societies, hire-purchase companies, and other organisations which provide credit to the private sector. The organisation exchanges information and records known fraud under the individual's name and address. This then allows companies to check applications against the information in the CIFAS database.

Police Co-operation

It is a fact of life for credit card companies that detecting fraud against businesses comes rather low down the list of priorities for most police forces. The police are generally not prepared to investigate this kind of alleged fraud. They will usually only be prepared to involve the Crown Prosecution Service if the card issuer has conducted its own thorough investigation and presents the evidence in the correct format.

If, however, a card issuer has other links with its local police (perhaps both the bank manager and the local chief of police are masons,) the issuer may be able to drum up rather more help. In general, where someone is charged with credit card fraud, this offence will appear way down a long list of other offences.

Even if the police are not usually over keen to help credit card companies in their investigations, it does sometimes happen the other way round. On one occasion some years ago, I had the job of handling my company's fraud reports. I came across one that showed a man sentenced to life imprisonment for credit card fraud among other crimes. While we welcome stiff penalties for fraudsters, this did seem a little extreme. However, it transpired that these "other crimes" included the murder of the man whose credit card he had stolen. In this instance, the murderer was tracked down, not by the police, but by the card issuer in the course of its own fraud investigations. The man who was killed had lived in Reading in Berkshire and the murderer fled, with the card, to Wales. When we started noticing heavy, unusual use of the card in the Principality, we became suspicious and informed the police. The police then arrested the man and, through his finger-prints, were able to link him with the killing.

Private Investigators

Private investigators can be used to track down fraudsters but their use can be expensive and often not successful. The quality of investigators varies greatly.

STATISTICS

Fraud levels are normally presented as a percentage of sales turnover of credit cards. There is usually a gross and a net fraud figure, because a card issuer will sometimes be able to recover some of the money lost.

The figures below are those published by VISA, but are thought to be reasonably representative of the UK credit card issuers as a whole.

	6-month average to 31/3/94 loss per £100 of sales	12-month average to 31/3/94 loss per £100 of sales
Credit cards		
Gross	16p	17p
Net	13p	15p
Debit cards		
Gross	10p	11p
Net	9p	10p

Some 14 per cent of losses are normally recovered; the difference between gross and net is, of course, the recoveries; card issuers will tend to hold auctions of recovered goods which were obtained fraudulently.

Fraud levels for debit cards are lower than for credit cards because the former tend to have a higher level of authorisation. However, the PFPF Committee (see above) is pushing for lower floor limits for credit cards, which would mean more of these transactions being subject to authorisation checks in an attempt to reduce further fraud levels.

At Save & Prosper, the overall level of fraud is around 0.1 per cent of sales turnover, compared with 0.16 per cent for VISA. This difference is largely accounted for by Save & Prospers's insistence of full documentation before an application is accepted. This documentation means it has a lower level of application fraud.

There are other indications which suggest that some fraud prevention methods can be highly effective. In May 1992, fraud levels were running at around 30p per £100 of sales, which shows that the PFPF initiative has reduced fraud levels by nearly half in two years.

Breakdown of fraud

By far the biggest area of fraud arises from lost and stolen cards.

Loss per £100 of sales (6–month average)

Stolen	0.12p
Card not received	0.02p
Counterfeit	0.01p
Other	0.01p
TOTAL	0.16p

The average loss per credit card per year is currently running at around £2.27 for each card in issue. (Which, interestingly, is broadly what it would cost to introduce photographs on to each card in issue.) There has been no counterfeit fraud recorded with debit cards. The average loss per debit card is lower at £2.07.

OTHER PREVENTION MEASURES

Personal Identification Numbers (PINs)

For all the media coverage of this area, I do not believe it is possible for a thief to obtain cash from an automated teller machine (ATM), without knowing the card-holder's PIN.

There are currently devices available which can "eavesdrop" on a customer using his PIN at an ATM to find out what is the number. But even here, the PIN is of no value unless the fraudster can get his hands on the card or card details as well.

The real danger is where customers have, say, their wallet stolen which contains both their card and a record of their PIN. To reduce the need for customers to write down their numbers (something they are expressly instructed never to do), many banks are now allowing them to choose their own number. The idea is simply that if a customer can select a number he finds easy to remember, there is no need for him to keep a written reminder, so that the risk of fraud is reduced.

Application fraud

A fraudster will often use an accommodation address when he applies for the card. What then generally happens is that the "customer" uses the card normally for a period – running up reasonable size debts and paying them off – before he embarks on a high level of spending and disappears. The accommodation address, which has been given as his home, makes him almost impossible to trace. However, the advent of CIFAS (see above), means that card issuers are sharing fraud information much more freely and suspect accommodation addresses are now more likely to be identified at the outset.

BAD DEBT

A bad debt arises where a customer, who has obtained his or her card perfectly legitimately, is later unable (because of a change in circumstances, for example) or unwilling to repay the amount he has borrowed on a credit card.

Each card issuer will take a slightly different policy to its handling of bad debts and, in each individual customer's case, the approach will depend on how long the account has been delinquent and the amount owing. Delinquent is the word used to describe accounts which are either above their credit limit, and/or where the customer has been failing to repay the minimum requirement each month.

For the purposes of illustration, we will run through a typical approach to bad debt. Not all card issuers will react in the same way; some will be more lenient, some harsher, but this provides an impression of what steps are available and why and when they will be taken.

Delinquency

If an account becomes delinquent, the card issuer will write to the customer telling him he is over his limit and asking him to stop using the card until it has been brought back into line. If the account belongs to a 'good' customer, with a history of prompt repayments, the issuer might automatically increase his credit limit. This would mean the "problem" has disappeared as far as the bank is concerned.

If, however, it is a customer who only ever pays off the minimum or who has been in arrears before, raising the limit is possibly the very worst thing the issuer could do. In this instance, the issuer would require the customer to bring his account back under the credit limit. If he failed to do so, the issuer would put a stop on authorising any further transactions – which would mean he would be unable to use his card. Ultimately, if the debt was not being repaid, the issuer would take steps to recover its money.

When an account goes into arrears – that is, no monthly payment has been made – the first statement after non-payment will include a gentle reminder that it is overdue. If, two weeks later, no payment is forthcoming, a letter will be sent. This will again remind the customer, and ask him not to use the card until he has caught up with his payments. At this stage, however, the issuer would not necessarily put a formal stop on his card.

By the end of the second month, which would mean around 35 days of arrears, the issuer will step up its pressure. It would stop authorising any further use of the card and write demanding payment of the amount in arrears. After a further two weeks of non-payment, the issuer would send a termination notice and demand payment of the debt in full within 14 days. A termination notice is where the issuer exercises its right to cancel the agreement and demand the return of the card and repayment of the debt.

Legal Action

At this stage, the action to follow would depend on the amount outstanding. If the sum is under £1,000, the issuer may call in debt collectors to try to recover the money. If, however, after six months, they have been unable to do so, the issuer may simply write off the debt.

If the amount is between £1,000 and £2,500, the issuer might seek to obtain a County Court Judgment against the errant customer. Once judgment has been obtained, the issuer can investigate whether the customer has enough equity in his house to cover the debt. If there is, the issuer can apply to the court for a charging order over the house. If this is granted, the issuer then applies for a possession order and may try to force the sale of the house. However, this is often not a straightforward process. If the credit card is in the customer's sole name, but his house is in joint names with his spouse, the spouse has a right to continue living in the house, despite the CCJ. In this instance, the issuer might try to persuade a judge that its right to obtain repayment outweighs the spouse's right to a home, but many judges are reluctant to accept such an argument.

Another course of action is to seek an attachment of earnings order. This means that money is automatically deducted from the customer's salary to repay the debt. Again, this can be problematic. If the customer is self-employed, it is not effective. Or, in some areas of work, an attachment of earnings may be so frowned on by an employer that it may mean the customer/employee loses his job. This is obviously self-defeating, as a customer is unlikely to be able to make any payments if he is out of work.

However, despite the practical problems, CCJs can be effective. If the customer is a professional person, the threat of proceedings and consequent damage they could do to his reputation, are often enough to persuade him to pay up.

If the amount outstanding is more than £2,500, the issuer could immediately issue a statutory demand for payment and proceed directly to bankruptcy. This course of action can be invoked for sums under this amount, but may not be considered a cost effective option as it is an expensive route to go. It is not possible to institute bankruptcy proceedings for accounts of less than £800, and it is certainly not cost–effective to do so unless you are certain the debtor has the resources to pay in full.

Customer Relationships

The steps we have outlined would be taken only if the customer had steadfastly refused to communicate with the bank and explain his or her problems. At every stage of the process, it is the issuer's intention to get him to agree with it, a realistic repayment plan. Where a debt has been run up in good faith but an individual's circumstances have changed, a bank is likely to look favourably on any realistic arrangements that can be worked out. However, if a customer agrees a repayment programme and then breaks the arrangement, the issuer may feel it appropriate to take legal action.

Once the process has been put on a legal footing, the issuer would be likely to deem the banking relationship to have broken down. Even if the individual subsequently repays the money, he is unlikely to be wanted any more as a customer. Nor would the issuer be likely to give a favourable bank reference. However, if the difficulty is sorted out without the need for recourse to law, the relationship may continue depending on the circumstances.

The catalyst for a bad debt is usually a change in the customer's circumstances; a fall in income or increase in expenditure caused, say, by illness, divorce, or unemployment. These are all events which mean a customer may not be able to pay back money he borrowed in the expectation that he would be able to service the debt.

Where circumstances have changed, issuers will tend to be sympathetic. However, sympathy is unlikely to be extended if the customer committed financial fraud – by overstating his income or understating his commitments – in his original application.

A customer who wishes to avoid bankruptcy can enter into an independent voluntary arrangement, handing over his assets and liabilities to an administrator. This official then asks all his creditors to agree to accept a percentage of what they are owed. Most issuers will generally go along with these arrangements, provided the customer has been acting in good faith. If he concealed his true financial situation at the outset, fraud has been committed and some issuers would choose to call in the police.

For example, a gardener employed by a local authority applied to his bank for a credit card. On his application form, he stated that he was employed as a manager, that he owned his own home, and claimed that he had no other credit commitments. He subsequently ran up debts with the bank of £4,000. It then transpired that he did not own his home and he owed around £260,000 to some 30 organisations. In this instance, the bank was not minded to come to any arrangement with him and called in the police! He was eventually sentenced to nine months in prison for fraud. It did not get the bank its money back, but it serves as a warning to other potential fraudsters.

The delinquency figures will vary from one credit card company to another. In general terms, however, they expect to write off as bad debts around 2-2.5 per cent of their lending. In 1994, around 6.5 per cent of a card issuers' outstanding lending is on delinquent accounts. Subsequently, some 1.5 per cent may be written off as bad debts. However, the remaining 4–5 per cent may be recovered.

EIGHT

THE LEGAL
FRAMEWORK

Introduction

The law relating to credit cards is extremely wide and complex. It includes the law of contract; the Consumer Credit Act 1974; the Sex Discrimination Act 1975; the Race Relations Act 1976; the Fair Trading Acts; and the Unfair Contracts Terms Act 1977; and the Data Protection Act 1984.

Credit card agreements can involve two, three or four parties. A store card, like the one operated by John Lewis, where the card issuer supplies the goods and services and also supplies the finance, is an example of a two-party agreement. (See Table A on page 82).

With a three-party agreement, there are the card issuer/merchant acquirer, the cardholder and the merchant. (See Table A on page 82.) The card issuing bank and the merchant acquiring bank are the same in this example.

A four-party agreement is where the issuing bank and the merchant acquiring bank are different. In this instance, you would have an agreement between the merchant acquirer and the merchant; and an agreement between the cardholder and the merchant (for the purpose of buying goods and services). The acquiring and issuing banks would normally both be members of the card organisation, say VISA or MasterCard. The rules of that organisation will require the card issuer to reimburse the merchant acquirer for transactions that the acquirer has made. (See Table A on page 82.)

Some banks issue and acquire; some banks issue only. There will not normally be a direct contract between an issuing and an acquiring bank, but both will be members of a payments organisation, such as VISA or MasterCard and agree to be bound by its rules and obligations.

Table A: Credit Card Agreements:

(a) A two–party agreement:

client ←——————→ retail store

(b) A three–party agreement:

Card issuer/Merchant acquiring bank ←——————→ cardholder

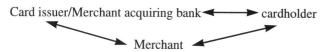

Merchant

(c) A four–party agreement:

Card issuer ←——→ VISA/MASTERCARD ←——→ Merchant acquiring bank

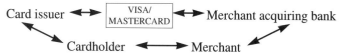

Cardholder ←——→ Merchant

It is, however, possible for the issuing and acquiring banks to enter into a local interchange agreement which varies the standard rules of the card organisation, be it VISA or MasterCard. For example, a different interchange rate or cash advance reimbursement fee might be agreed.

Arrangements between the parties are bound by the general law of contract, and by the legislation which specifically relates to credit cards.

Cardholder agreements

The basic law of contract applies to cardholder agreements. Under this, legal agreements need to satisfy six basic criteria:

- consensus of the parties (offer and acceptance)

- consideration (money, or some other valuable consideration)

- capacity (the parties must be able legally to contract)

- formality (the document must be correct)

- legality (the purpose of the contract must be legal)

- intention to contract (the parties must share the same intention).

A typical bank card contract may contain some or all of the following clauses:

a) The card must be signed by the cardholder and can be used by that card-holder only. It must be used subject to the conditions of use applicable, including remaining within the credit limit set by the issuer.

b) The issuer will debit the account with the amount that the cardholder has spent using the card. The cardholder must pay his bank the debited amounts within a specified period after the date of the statement, whether or not he signed a sales voucher. Claims by a cardholder against a merchant cannot be offset or counterclaimed against the issuer, except to the extent that S75 of the Consumer Credit Act 1974 applies.

c) Daily interest will be charged on the outstanding balance and will be debited from the account the following month. If the full amount is repaid by the due date, normally no interest is payable. However, cash advances may be subject to a handling charge, or be subject to interest from the date of the advance until it is repaid in full.

d) The cardholder must make at least the minimum payment each month. If, however, there is any breach of the conditions of use, the full amount becomes payable immediately. The issuer also has the discretion to seek full repayment in the event of the cardholder's bankruptcy, voluntary arrangement with creditors or death, subject, of course, to any statutory considerations.

e) The card remains the property of the issuer. The cardholder can end the agreement at any time without notice by returning his card to the issuer.

f) If a card is lost or stolen, the cardholder must immediately notify the bank. His liability is limited to a maximum of £50 of amounts debited before notification.

g) The issuer has no liability if a card is not honoured by a supplier.

Most of these clauses are reasonably self-explanatory, although it is useful to be aware of the reasons which underlie some of them. For example, clause b) determines that a cardholder cannot avoid having to pay for goods simply because a shop assistant forgot to ask him to sign a sales voucher. The fact that he presented his card is enough for his account to be debited with the amount of genuine purchases. It also allows cards to be used for over-the-phone purchases. If there is a dispute between the cardholder and the supplier, the cardholder cannot stop paying (although he may have rights against the card company if the goods are faulty, as we discuss in Chapter Seven).

Clauses c) and d) are strictly contractual and statute law does not apply. However, the Government may, from time to time, intervene by specifying minimum monthly repayments. This happened in the 1970s, when the Government increased the minimum repayment from 5 per cent to 15 per cent of the amount owing.

Clause e) specifies that the card remains the property of the issuer. This means that where a company wants to stop someone using the card – be it the holder who is spending way over his limit or an unauthorised user – it can demand that the card is returned. Similarly, the cardholder can terminate the agreement by giving back his card, and paying off the balance.

Clause f) reflects Section 84 of the Consumer Credit Act 1974 which limits the cardholder's liability in the event of mis-use by another person to £50. This is the maximum figure allowed, although there is nothing to stop an issuer imposing a lesser charge.

In the past, issuers would routinely pass on information about cardholders to their agents and other parts of their organisation. However, this practice now contravenes the Code of Banking Practice. This dictates that banks can only pass on information with the express permission of the cardholder. The Data Protection Act also has an impact in this area. Under this Act, information can only be used for the purpose for which it was given, unless the cardholder has given his or her permission for it to be passed on.

All agreements must comply with the Consumer Credit (Agreements) Regulations 1983 issued under the Consumer Credit Act 1974. These Regulations set out what information must appear in an agreement, and in what form.

Most credit card agreements are multiple agreements encompassing both debtor-creditor-supplier agreements, as well as debtor-creditor agreements. The former covers the situation where a credit card is used to pay for goods and services in a shop displaying a VISA or MasterCard sign. The latter covers the situation where a card is used to obtain cash from a bank. In the former situation, the cardholder may receive protection offered by Section 75 of the Consumer Credit Act in respect of transactions between £100 and £15,000 (see below).

To comply with the Agreements Regulations an agreement must:

- be in the prescribed form and be signed in the prescribed manner;

- embody all the terms of the agreement, other than the implied terms;

- be readily legible when presented to the cardholder for signature.

Five main types of information must be given:

1   The heading.

"A Credit Agreement regulated by the Consumer Credit Act 1974." – which reflects the nature of the agreement;

2   The name and address of each party.

This must include the full name of any limited company, partnership or individual and full postal addresses must be given;

3   Financial details.

These must be shown "together and whole". This means that all the financial information required to be included must be set out in one part of the agreement (known colloquially as the "holy ground"), with no other information being inserted in that part.

The main financial details which must be included are:

a)   the credit limit;

b)   the interest rate and amount of other charges;

c)   the timing and amounts of repayments;

d)   the annual percentage rate (APR) and whether or not the interest rate can be varied and in what circumstances, such as at the discretion of the bank.

4   A description of any direct security or default charges.

Any security given by the debtor must be briefly described and the relevant security document referred to. Security given by third parties only, need not be mentioned although third-party security may be a precondition of the facility. It may, therefore, be mentioned as a term of the agreement. However, secured credit card lending has yet to migrate to the UK from the US.

Any fees or other charges payable on default must be described outside the "holy ground".

5   Cancellation notices.

These must be given equal prominence to the other terms of the agreement.

Apart from the above five categories of information, other terms may be included in the agreement so long as they are not given more prominence than the statutory heading, the APR or the statutory notices; and so long as they are not inserted in the "holy ground".

Agreements can also be "cancellable" or "non-cancellable". An agreement is non-cancellable if there has been no oral communication between the card issuer and the cardholder during the application process – if the applicant simply picked up an application form from his local branch, completed it and sent it in. If, however, there has been verbal contact between them –say, a bank official spoke to the customer over the telephone about his application – it is a cancellable agreement. This means that the cardholder can terminate the agreement up to seven days after his application has been accepted. In theory, this could mean a cardholder using his new card, then cancelling the arrangement and leaving the bank in some difficulties to recover its funds – because there would be no live contract between them.

Agreements also have to include a clause setting out the process by which its terms can be varied. These include giving the cardholder reasonable notice and publicising in two national newspapers notification of any changes in interest rates charged. In practice, most issuers give at least a month's notice of any change in rates.

Issuers generally include a clause giving them the right to terminate the agreement without notice, although this is only likely to be exercised if the account is being misused.

Merchant Agreement

The basic terms in a merchant agreement are fairly straightforward. Disputes between issuer with either cardholders or merchants are rare. The most common areas of discord between merchant and issuer are probably claims by merchants over the appropriate level of merchant service charge (or discount) and problems arising from wrongly completed vouchers which mean the card company cannot identify the cardholder.

A merchant agreement will usually include the following terms;

- the merchant will accept all cards of a particular type (eg. VISA) up to the "floor limit" specified. For transactions above the floor limit, the merchant will seek authorisation and record the authorisation code on the voucher. The floor limit is the amount established for single transactions at specific types of merchant outlets, above which authorisation is required;

- the merchant will check the card is still valid – that it has not expired, and that it does not appear on the stop list issued by the card company;

- the merchant will use only the sales vouchers in a format agreed with the card company. He will ensure the customer signs the voucher and will give him a copy. The merchant will ensure that his identification number appears on the voucher;

- the merchant will claim reimbursement promptly, less the agreed merchant service charge. The time limits are usually three days for VISA and MasterCard/Access; ten days for Amex; and Diners prefers weekly but will allow up to 30 days;

- the merchant's bank account will be credited with the sum of sales less discount, subject to rejection by the card company of any invalid vouchers;

- refunds will be made by refund vouchers and deducted from the amount claimed by the merchant acquiring bank. No reasonable request for a refund by a cardholder will be refused by a merchant simply because goods were paid for with a credit card;

- the merchant can charge any extra for goods bought with a credit card, or, alternatively, offer a discount for payment by cash or cheque.

The presentation of sales vouchers for payment by the card company shall be a warranty that:–

a) the information supplied is correct;

b) the merchant has supplied goods or services to the value stated, goods have been supplied at the cash price and there is no element of credit for any other purpose;

c) the provision of credit for the supply of goods or services in respect of which a sales voucher is issued is lawful.

- the merchant irrevocably authorises the card company to debit his bank account with sums which are payable in respect of:

a) the merchant service charge;

b) VAT on the merchant service charge;

c) refunds to cardholders;

d) the value of sales vouchers issued in breach of the terms;

e) interest at an agreed percentage over base rate on any sums not paid by the merchant;

f) any other sums due to the merchant acquiring bank.

- the agreement is not assignable. In the case of individuals, it also binds their representatives;

- the agreement may be terminated at a specified period of notice on either side. The equipment supplied remains the property of the merchant acquiring bank and must be returned.

The merchant agreement will also specify circumstances where a sales voucher will be invalid. These would include where:

- the transaction is illegal;

- the signature obtained does not match the one on the card;

- there is a discrepancy between the sales voucher given to the customer and the one supplied to the bank, or it is incomplete;

- the value of the transaction is above the floor limit and has not been authorised;

- the terms of the merchant's agreement have been broken;

- the card has expired;

- the card has been listed as void by the issuer.

There are various ways in which a transaction can become void the most important of which are if the expiry date has passed or if the signatures do not match.

Amex and Diners include in their merchant agreements the right to debit back to the merchant any amount which the cardholder disputes and refuses to pay. Amex also specifies that merchants must settle disputes within 30 days (so long as the cardholder behaves reasonably and in good faith).

Both Amex and Diners also try to insist that their logos and other advertisements are displayed prominently. Amex insists that merchants do not accept payment direct from a customer where the purchase has been made by Amex card (but that merchants endorse cheques to Amex). In the case of car hire, the Amex agreement used to specify that Amex customers would not be required to sign a blank voucher prior to hire – although this requirement was frequently flouted in practice, and now seems to have been dropped.

Diners draw attention in its retailer agreement to the reward offered for recovery of lost or stolen cards and insists that its list of hot cards is treated as confidential. It also specifies a lengthy period of notice of termination to allow time for the merchant's name to be deleted from the Diners' directory.

*

Advertising and quotations

There are three broad types of advertisements: simple, intermediate and full.

Simple advertisements

Simple advertisements are where, for lack of space or reader's time, the advertiser can put over only a brief message. The only information which can be shown is the advertiser's name, logo, address, telephone number and occupation. It may mention that the advertiser is willing to extend credit but no other information other than the cash price of any goods, services and other things.

Intermediate advertisements

Some basic credit information can be given. An advertisement of this type must include the following details:

- the advertiser's name;
- the advertiser's address or telephone number;
- if applicable, a statement that security or insurance is required;
- if applicable, a statement that a sum of money must be deposited in an account;
- if applicable, any credit-broker's fee payable;
- where the cash price is given in the advertisement, the APR should be quoted indicating if the rate of interest may vary;
- a statement that written quotations are available.

The advertiser may show other optional information, but no information may be shown indicating that a card issuer is prepared to provide credit other than as follows:

(a) the card issuer's logo (or that of his trade association);

(b) the general nature of the card issuer's business;

(c) a statement that credit facilities are available;

(d) whether the facilities are restricted to any class or group;

(e) if the APR is not already stated as part of the compulsory information, it may be stated together with the rate of interest;

(f) the amount of credit which may be granted;

(g) the nature of any security required where it does not comprise of a mortgage on the debtor's home;

(h) if the APR is stated, then details of any advance payment must also be stated;

(i) the name, address and telephone number of the card issuer must be stated, if the optional information indicates that credit facilities are available.

Of course, in practise card issuers do not normally require security, insurance or a deposit before issuing cards. It would be most unusual for a credit broker to be involved.

Full advertisements

If the advertiser wants to give more information than is allowable in an intermediate advertisement, he must publish a full advertisement. The Regulations governing full advertisements aim to ensure that the customer is given a full and fair picture of the credit that is on offer.

These include "representative terms", designed to ensure that credit limits, repayment terms and so on are likely to reflect what happens in practice. Where applicable, the statutory warnings must be included.

The following information must be included in full credit advertisements:

(a) the name and address of the card issuer;

(b) an indication of whether security is required – in practice it is not;

(c) an indication of whether insurance is required – in practice it is not;

(d) an indication if a deposit is required – in practice it is not;

(e) details of any fee payable by the debtor to a credit broker – in practice there is not;

(f) a statement that the individuals may request a written quotation about the terms of the agreement;

(g) the APR;

(h) whether the offer is restricted to a class or group of persons – in practice it will not be;

(i) the nature of security required not affecting the debtor's home – in practice no security will be required;

(j) the frequency, number and amount of advance payments expressed either as a sum of money or as a percentage – in practice none will be required;

(k) an indication if there is different treatment of cash and credit purchases – in practice this can usually be ignored;

(l) the frequency, number and amount of repayments required;

(m) details of any other charges such as annual card fees.

There are a few other requirements, but these do not apply to debtor–credit–supplier agreements i.e. credit card lending.

Quotations

A quotation is intended to give the prospective customer an indication of how much the credit on offer is likely to cost him. There are Regulations governing the form and contents of these quotations. The Consumer Credit (Quotations) Regulations 1989 prescribe the circumstances in which a quotation may be sought – by whom, from whom, when and how often. For example, a second quotation on the same transaction cannot be sought within 28 days of the original request. A minor or foreign resident cannot request a quotation.

The information that must be supplied with a quotation is similar to that for an intermediate advertisement, plus the credit limit and repayment details.

The Office of Fair Trading has recommended to the Department of Trade and Industry that the Quotations Regulations be scrapped.

Annual percentage rate of interest (APR)

The Consumer Credit (Total Charge for Credit) Regulations 1980 set out the rules for calculating the rate of the total charge for credit, known as the annual percentage rate of interest, or APR.

The APR was introduced as a means by which customers can easily compare the cost of credit from different providers. However, while it may work reasonably well with other types of credit, it can give a misleading impression when applied to credit cards.

In calculating APR, you need to take into account both the interest rate and all other charges incurred with the card, such as the annual membership fee. However, the current Regulations do not allow you to take into account any interest-free period that is being granted to customers.

When calculating APR, you have to assume that interest is going to be paid immediately that the transaction is notified to the bank – which is clearly not what happens in practice with many cards. This shortcoming means that you can have two issuers, one of which has an interest-free period, the other does not, yet if they both charge the same monthly rate of interest, they can both quote the same APR. This, despite the fact that borrowing from the latter company will cost customers more.

The Royal Bank of Scotland, MasterCard, for example, does not have an interest-free period. So, in relation to other issuers that do, its APR is understated.

Even where issuers do allow an interest-free period, there can still be variations. It may begin from the date the transaction appears on the statement or, more commonly now, from the date it reaches the bank. Even this kind of variation can have an impact on the cost of borrowing. However, credit card advertisements are not required to spell out the details of any interest-free period.

Another way the APR can be manipulated is in the assumption of the amount to be borrowed, particularly where an annual card fee is charged. If, say, you have an annual charge of £10 and you assume the amount to be borrowed is £250, that £10 has to be spread across £250. If, however, you assume the amount borrowed is £2,500, the card fee is going to have a far lesser effect on the APR.

A better guide than the APR would be for credit card companies to be required to tell consumers what it would cost in £s to borrow, say, £1,000 for a year. In any event, most consumers do not understand what the APR means.

The Office of Fair Trading has made recommendations to the Department of Trade and Industry that the APR formula be changed to exclude any card charge which in future should be disclosed separately.

Connected lender liability

The connected lender liability provisions – Section 75 – are probably the most contentious section of the Consumer Credit Act. It is a provision originally intended to cover specific credit transactions which also caught credit card transactions. It effectively requires credit card issuers to underwrite the entire UK retail sector for all transactions of £100 to £15,000. The provision stipulates that if a consumer buys goods or services under a debtor-creditor-supplier agreement, the card issuer is liable to the cardholder in the event of the goods or services not being delivered, or if they are unsatisfactory.

If goods have been ordered, but the supplier goes out of business before they are delivered, the issuer has to step in to compensate the customer. If the goods are unsatisfactory, the cardholder has the right to take proceedings against the issuer for compensation. If the merchant is still trading, the issuer can ask that the merchant is joined to the action so that both become parties to the action.

Some of the claims that are made under this provision can be bizarre to say the least. A man bought a £1,000 orthopaedic bed which it was claimed would help bad back sufferers. When it failed to help his back, he tried to sue the card issuer. Another customer bought a second–hand television on his VISA card. He, too, asked his bank for a refund because he had believed he was buying a set with remote control which it turned out not to have.

An issuer may successfully fend off this type of spurious claim, but still has to waste time and money in corresponding with such customers.

Another problem with Section 75 claims is its jurisdiction. It is not yet clear whether it applies to transactions conducted outside the UK. The banking ombudsman believes that Section 75 is not applicable where goods have been bought overseas. However, the Director General of Fair Trading takes the view that it does. This matter is still to be finally resolved. But, from a practical point of view, it is difficult to see how any bank in London can be expected to have control over goods supplied by merchants recruited, say, in Singapore or Moscow.

Further, a card issuer is liable under Section 75 for the entire price of the goods, even if it was only the deposit that was paid for on the card.

Debit cards, however, are not subject to Section 75 because they are used to access a current account (even though that account might have an overdraft facility). Similarly, charge cards are exempt from Section 75 liability because the holder is required to settle his account in full at the end of each month.

Unsolicited card issue

Under Section 51, it is an offence to issue an unsolicited credit card. This restriction was introduced after the launch of Access, when three million unsolicited cards were distributed. It is also an offence to issue a credit card to a minor, or to send a mailshot to a minor encouraging him or her to apply for a card.

Credit brokerage

Credit brokerage is where an individual who needs credit is introduced to an organisation which provides the credit. An introducer – who brokers on a regular basis – needs to have a licence granted by the Director General of Fair Trading.

The types of credit involved are:

- regulated credit;

- exempt credit, unless it falls under the exemptions because of the number of repayments;

- credit secured on land where the individual wants the credit to buy a house for himself or a relative;

- a credit agreement governed by foreign law, but which would be regulated by the act if governed under UK law.

For example, where a retailer helps a customer fill out a personal loan application form for some of his goods and then sends the form to a finance company for approval, the retailer would need to be licensed. In this instance, he is clearly introducing a customer to a source of credit.

However, where merchants merely advertise that they accept specific payment cards – say, VISA or MasterCard – they do not need a credit licence. The merchants are not introducing shoppers to the banks which issue payment cards. There is an important distinction to be made between assisting someone to take credit under his existing agreement and introducing him to a prospective credit supplier.

A bank which uses a third party to market or sell its loan facilities must ensure that the third party holds a credit licence where necessary. If a customer enters into a regulated agreement following an introduction from an unlicensed credit broker, the agreement will only be enforceable at the discretion of the Director General of Fair Trading. In reaching his decision, the Director General will take into account how far the debtor was prejudiced by the broker's conduct; and the degree of culpability of the creditor in enabling the credit broker to carry on business without a licence.

Where appropriate, credit brokers must provide prospective borrowers with quotations, in accordance with the relevant regulations.

Canvassing and circulars

Credit cards cannot generally be marketed door-to-door. A card issuer cannot employ salespeople to visit potential customers' homes unannounced to try to entice them to apply for a card. However, a credit card salesperson can go to a customer's home if he has been expressly invited to do so.

Card issuers can, however, make unsolicited telephone and written approaches to potential customers encouraging them to take out a card.

Review of the Consumer Credit Act 1974

The Department of Trade and Industry has requested the Office of Fair Trading to review certain aspects of the Act. It is possible that there may be changes to the Act - particularly in relation to the calculation of APRs and Section 75: connected lender liability.

NINE

CARD OPERATIONS :
THE PROFIT AND LOSS ACCOUNT

There are two distinct sides to this aspect: the costs and income associated with issuing cards; and the costs and income associated with merchant acquiring. Even where a bank is both issuer and acquirer, the two sides of the business will tend to be run separately. Whereas, in the early 1980s, no distinction would have to be made between the two.

Sources of income for card issuers

Joining fee

A joining fee is a one-off charge a cardholder has to pay when he first applies for his card. These charges are more usually associated with gold cards, rather than standard credit cards.

Annual card fees

Many issuers charge the cardholder an annual fee for having the card. Some issuers like the TSB, however, do not impose this fee. The Co-operative Bank offers a free-for-life gold card, with a minimum number of transactions required each year. If a cardholder fails to meet this number, the Co–op retains the right to impose a fee, but has not yet done so.

Interest

The amount of interest received from cardholders depends on the prevailing interest rate at the time and on the proportion of outstanding balances on which interest is paid.

Where a customer settles his or her account in full each month, he will not incur an interest cost. Therefore, that proportion of lending does not earn interest for the card issuer. On average in the UK, 40 per cent of outstanding balances do not earn interest. For example, if a card issuer has, say, £100m outstanding, only £60m of that will earn interest. This means that the amount of interest a bank charges does not actually represent the total amount of money it will receive.

If a bank were charging, say, 1.5 per cent a month interest, it would, in fact, receive only 60 per cent of that 1.5 per cent, or 0.9 per cent of the amount outstanding. Therefore, taking our previous £100m as the total outstanding, an interest rate of 1.5 per cent a month represents not £1.5m, but £900,000 of interest earned.

This is a crucial factor to grasp and is fundamental to the profitability of the credit card operation. In general terms, the higher the proportion of lending that is interest bearing – and this can vary substantially from issuer to issuer – the greater the profitability.

Merchant service fee

The merchant service fee is the fee paid by the merchant to the merchant acquiring bank. The interchange fee is the sum which is paid by the merchant acquiring bank to the issuer for sales transactions. The difference between the merchant service fee and the interchange fee accrues to the merchant acquiring bank.

In the UK, this is on average about 1.1 per cent of the value of the sale. Therefore, for every £100 spend on a card, the card issuing bank will receive £1.10.

In practice, the amount paid will vary according to whether a transaction is electronic and authorised, or paper-based and unauthorised. Electronic transactions generally attract a lower interchange fee rate than paper-based, unauthorised transactions.

Cash advance fee

The cash advance fee is paid by the cardholder when he obtains cash using the card. Most issuers will charge 1.5 per cent of the amount obtained. Some will impose a minimum fee, say £2 per transaction. Others may not impose a fee, but simply charge interest from the date the cash is taken, dispensing with their usual interest-free period; or a bank may impose a fee, and charge interest from the next statement date, if the amount has not been settled in full by then. Yet other issuers will charge both a fee and charge interest from the date the cash is taken.

Default charges

It is now usual for issuers to impose a charge on the customer if he goes over his credit limit or is in arrears with his payments.

Costs incurred by card issuers

Costs of funds

If a card issuer is lending money to customers, it has itself to borrow that money from somewhere, and pay interest for the privilege. Normally, card issuers use the seven-day or three-month London Inter-bank Offer (LIBOR) rate as the measure of the cost of raising the deposits it needs to enable it to lend to cardholders.

Let us assume an inter-bank rate of, say, 5.25 per cent. The interest being charged by the bank to its customers is 1.5 per cent a month; and 60 per cent of its outstanding lending is interest-earning. This card issuer would, therefore, expect to earn around £10.8m in interest income. The difference between the cost of funds and gross interest earned – that is, the 5.25 per cent interest rate on the £100m that is outstanding, versus the £10.8m interest you are earning – is known as the net interest earned, or as the net interest margin.

Net interest margin on outstandings of £100m.

Monthly rate	% Interest earning				Annual rate		£m
1.5 % x 60% x 12				=	10.8%	=	10.80
Inter-bank rate				=	5.25%	=	5.25
Net interest margin				=	5.55%	=	5.55

Fraud

Fraud is usually calculated as a percentage of cardholder sales volume. In the UK, on average, fraud currently runs at about 0.16 per cent of sales volume. This means that for every £100 spent on a credit card, you would expect 16p to be fraudulent.

Bad debts

Card issuers normally build up provision to cover anticipated bad debts. The issuer would calculate that it expects x per cent of its existing lending to go bad. It would, therefore, make provision to cover this amount and charge this to its profit and loss account at the time the lending takes place.

When individual cases of bad debt materialise, this is then charged against the earlier provision. The issuer then has to decide whether the remaining provision is sufficient to cover outstanding lending.

For example, an issuer has £100m-worth of lending. It is calculated that 2 per cent of this will go bad. The issuer, therefore, needs to provide £2m for bad

97

debts. If then during the course of the year, £0.5m actually goes bad and has to be written off, this amount is then charged to the provision. Bad debt provision has now dropped to £1.5m. The issuer then has to ask itself whether this lower figure is enough to cover the rest of the year. If it is, that is the end of the matter and there is no further charge to the profit and loss account in the short term. If the provision is thought to be inadequate, the £1.5m will need to be topped up and the amount by which this is done is charged to the profit and loss account.

The amount of provision card issuers allow for bad debts will vary with the state of the economy. When times are good, it will tend to be lower; when times are bad, more people are likely to default and the issuer needs to respond accordingly. At the time of writing (September 1994), most issuers have a fairly large bad debt provision. If the economy really is set to continue to improve, the issuers may be able to reduce their bad debt provision. They may find they have over-provided and be able to credit some money back to their profit and loss accounts.

Apart from the state of the economy, there are other factors which determine what proportion of an issuer's lending has to be written off. This will also be influenced by issues such as the bank's credit control and debt recovery systems.

During 1993, on average, card issuers issuing VISA cards wrote off 0.54 per cent of their sales volume. This translates into bad debt write offs of around 1.4 per cent of lending.

Section 75 claims

Under Section 75 of the Consumer Credit Act 1974, card issuers have obligations to cardholders to reimburse them for the cost of goods bought on the card which turn out to be faulty, or do not materialise. These payments do not tend to be that numerous, or very significant in comparison with other related costs. However, they can be expensive in terms of management time.

Staff costs

A card issuer will need to employ staff to perform a whole range of functions associated with its business. These would include card review, credit scoring, debt recovery, fraud prevention and client services.

A large-scale card issuer would normally expect to have to employ something in the range of 18-20 staff members for every 200,000 accounts. Smaller operators, however, would not be able to achieve this level of economy of scale and, consequently, employ relatively more staff.

Information systems

Information systems are a significant proportion of any card issuers total costs. This is not just a case of running a computer system, but of constantly enhancing it to meet the mandatory requirements imposed by VISA and MasterCard, as well as those necessitated by keeping up with the competition.

It is estimated that card issuers need to put in between 12-20 man years into system amendments every year.

Fees paid to international card payment organisations

These are the fees paid to VISA, MasterCard and Europay for membership and use of their payment networks.

Cash advance reimbursement fees

Card issuers will need to pay fees to other banks in return for them providing cash to their cardholders. The VISA cash advance reimbursement fee is currently $1.75, plus 0.33 per cent of the amount of cash taken. Fees of this kind can be a substantial cost, particularly if a card issuer does not have a cash dispenser or branch network of its own.

Premises

Quite clearly, a card issuer or a merchant acquirer needs premises in which to house its staff. Generally, the closer the operation to London, the more expensive the cost of premises.

Marketing

Every card issuer will have some kind of budget allocated to marketing to help generate new cardholders. In general terms, the level of cost will depend on the methods used to try to attract business.

If a card issuer has a well-established branch network, the marginal costs of new business may be very low. It might be able to rely on training its staff to spot potential customers and providing leaflets in its branches. In this situation, the costs of running the branch would be being incurred anyway, with little additional expenditure involved.

If, however, an issuer relies on advertising to drum up new cardholders, the costs can be substantial. Save & Prosper spends around £10 on advertising per inquiry generated. Around 40 per cent of these inquirers go on to become cardholders, which works out at around £25 spent on advertising for each new account. Many banks would expect to spend around double that amount for each new customer.

Direct mail is another marketing method often used by card issuers. To make it cost effective, a bank needs to achieve a response rate of 2-3 per cent which, with the availability of sophisticated databases, is realistically achievable.

Cardholder services

Issuers have the expense of posting monthly statements of account, processing payments to accounts, and dealing with cardholder payments. These, on average, cost £12 a year for each account.

Sources of income for merchant acquirers

Merchant service charge

The merchant service charge is the fee imposed by the acquirer on the merchant. It is usually based on a proportion of the value of each sales transaction – often 1-3 per cent. The actual amount charged will depend on the volume of business the merchant can supply to the acquirer: the higher the turnover, the lower the fee.

The level at which it is set will also be influenced by whether sales information is transmitted by the merchant to the acquirer electronically, or by using a paper-based system – with the former attracting a lower rate because it is less labour intensive for the acquirer. It will also depend on the level of fraud associated with that particular sector – the greater the risk, the greater the fee.

Income from the sale or rental of sales terminals to merchants

This will produce relatively minor revenue flows.

Costs incurred by merchant acquirers

Interchange fee

The interchange fee is paid by the merchant acquirer fee to the bank issuing the card. This is set at between 0.6-1.3 per cent of sales turnover, depending on whether or not the transaction is electronic.

Fees paid to international payment card organisations

Merchant acquirers have to pay fees to VISA, MasterCard and Europay for handling transactions and authorisation requests. They can expect to pay less than a penny per transaction.

Bad debts

Bad debts are incurred where the merchant fails to pay the merchant service charge. This is a phenomenon which can occur not infrequently particularly during recession, with many merchants experiencing financial problems.

Costs associated with rejected transactions

In theory, if a transaction is not accepted by the issuer, the merchant where it originated in the first place is liable for the cost. However, in some instances, the merchant acquirer may choose to absorb the cost itself. For instance, if a large group of companies, which does high volumes of credit card business, has breached the card acceptance rules in some minor way, the acquirer may bear the cost itself for the sake of maintaining a harmonious business relationship.

Staff costs

Like the card issuer, the acquirer will need to employ staff acting in a range of capacities. These would include having a sales force on the road, servicing merchants, staff dealing with queries arising from merchants and in processing transactions, an authorisation service, and running information systems. Many acquirers still rely on manual processing of transactions, which can make it labour intensive and expensive, although they are striving to automate this process.

Information systems

Again, like the card issuers, the acquirers have to fund the cost of updating and maintaining a computer system, much of which will involve mandatory requirements imposed by VISA and MasterCard.

Premises

Just like the issuers (see above), merchant acquirers need to house their staff and equipment. The costs vary according to location and the state of the property market.

TEN

TECHNOLOGY

Background

When credit cards were first introduced in the UK, the entire processing system was paper based.

Cards were embossed with the holder's details, but were not encoded on the magnetic stripe as they are now. For every transaction, the card had to be put through an imprinter, which manually transferred the details from it on to a paper slip. If the transaction needed to be authorised, the merchant had to make a telephone call to the merchant acquiring bank and ask for authorisation. If the card had been issued by a different bank, the merchant acquiring bank would, in turn, have to telephone that other bank/card issuer for authorisation.

Not surprisingly, verification could be an inordinately lengthy process and tended to be restricted to high value transactions. Once the paper transaction slip reached the bank, again it was processed manually.

Such a labour intensive process was only sustainable when the total volume of credit card transactions was relatively low. Once the number of credit cards in circulation began to increase, the banks and the merchants needed to find new, quicker ways of capturing the data.

Data capture

When the number of credit card transactions started to build, the banks began to encode the magnetic stripe with card number details and other information. The merchants began to install terminals which could automatically read these details. If authorisation is required for a particular transaction, because it is above a certain value, the terminal automatically telephones the merchant acquiring bank. In this way, authorisation can now be obtained in a matter of seconds, which also opens up the potential for far more transactions to be checked in this way.

The magnetic stripe has become the dominant way of reading data from a card. However, a considerable number of retail outlets still rely on manually transferring data and manual verification.

Signature vs PIN

In the UK, credit card transactions are signature, rather than Personal Identification Number (PIN), based. This means that the merchant still has the responsibility for deciding whether the signature on the sales slip corresponds to the signature on the card.

In France, however, where chip cards are in wide circulation, PINs are generally used. This negates the need for the merchant to verify the signature. Where a foreign-issued, and so non-chip card is used in France, the merchant still has to check the signature. There have been some instances of French merchants saying "non" to non-chip cards.

Bank processing

Where a merchant is capturing the data from a transaction electronically, this information can be transmitted to the bank electronically. Although the customer is still given a paper record of the purchase, a paper record is not actually sent to the bank.

Electronic information is far easier for the banks to handle and they will generally charge a reduced merchant service fee to outlets which transmit data in this way to reflect the lower processing costs involved.

As we have said (see above), a significant number of merchants still rely on manual processing. Even though this information will arrive at the bank in paper form, the bank is still able to process much of it automatically (rather than electronically) using imaging technology. An image is taken of the paper record, which is then fed into a computer. If the handwriting on the transaction slip is clear, the computer will be able to read it from the image. Where the writing is less clear, the computer may still be able to make sense of it. It can be programmed to effectively make a decision: what is the probability of this figure that looks vaguely like, say, a seven, being a seven? If it concludes that the probability is above a certain level, the computer will work on the basis that it is a seven and process the transaction accordingly. If the probability is below a certain figure, it will reject the transaction and ask an operator to check the voucher.

In France, even before chip cards were introduced, banks were still able to process transactions automatically. Instead of writing in the value of the transaction, merchants used imprinters into which they could key the amount, which would then be printed on the voucher, along with the details embossed on the card itself. When the vouchers reached the banks, therefore, they were able to be dealt with automatically in the way described above.

Magnetic stripes vs integrated circuit (or "chip") cards (ICC)

It is now generally accepted that magnetic stripes are yesterday's technology. They have been around for 25 years and suffer from not being fraud proof. It is a relatively simple procedure for a fraudster with a little knowledge to copy the information from one magnetic stripe on to another card. This security failing is one reason why the UK has been reluctant to switch away from signatures to PINs. At least with a signature, there is the additional safeguard of checking this against the signature on the card.

A number of anti-fraud devices have been developed to try to make magnetic stripes more secure. These include the card verification value (see Chapter Seven), and the use of watermarks. Barclays and NatWest, on behalf of VISA, are testing the use of watermarks on the magnetic stripe. The system should be able to detect whether data has been transferred from one magnetic stripe with a particular watermark on to another card with a different watermark or no watermark at all on its magnetic stripe.

For security reasons, PINs can only be used in conjunction with magnetic stripe cards if the number is encrypted while it is being transmitted from the point of sale to the card issuer for checking. If the PIN is not scrambled, ie encrypted, it would be relatively easy for a fraudster to intercept the transmission and use this in conjunction with a fake card created by transferring the data from the magnetic stripe.

With ICC cards, the chip is embedded into the card itself. Chip cards have to be used in conjunction with a merchant's terminal that can read the information in the chip. There are two ways in which a chip can be deciphered: using a contact terminal reader; or a contactless terminal reader. The former method involves the reader physically coming into contact with the chip, and is the more reliable of the two technologies. The latter, more sophisticated, method utilises a radio signal which reads the chip.

Contactless terminal readers are generally regarded to be suitable only for closed user environments, ie. in a factory canteen where workers are given chip cards which equate to a certain amount of cash. For open payment environments, such as general retail use, this type of reader is likely to fail too often to be acceptable.

Chip cards are generally used in conjunction with a PIN, rather than with signature verification. These cards are designed to "self destruct" if they are tampered with, which makes them far harder to duplicate.

Far more information can be stored on a chip than a magnetic stripe. This does not have just to be financial information; it could include the holder's address, date of birth, even his medical details or next of kin. Information can be divided up into sections, for example, one section for details relevant to the bank or card issuer, and another with personal information and perhaps a third for international payment links.

Although, as we have said, chip cards are not yet in general use in the UK, there is little doubt that it is only a matter of time before they are widely available. When they are, they will have to be accompanied by internationally accepted standards governing their implementation and use. So far, France is the only country to have developed the chip card into general use and this was only achieved after a heavy government subsidy. However, it seems unlikely that the standards used in France will be acceptable internationally and new ones are expected to be developed by the other countries. In this case, if France wants to be compatible with the rest of the world, its banking community will need to change its standards accordingly.

VISA and MasterCard are already working together to develop standards to which they will adhere, and it seems likely that these will be the ones adopted internationally. A trial of chip cards is expected to begin in the UK within two years, and a switch to chip cards is expected before the end of the century.

Chip cards are considerably more expensive than magnetic stripe cards – at probably around five times the cost. Each chip is currently reckoned to cost around £1.50/£2.00 compared with 30p for a magnetic stripe. Clearly, once chip cards start to be produced on a mass scale, the cost will come down. But they will still remain considerably more expensive than magnetic stripe cards.

There is, however, what is known as the "cheap chip", which has fewer facilities than the full-blown chip. The current thinking is that the banks will not opt to go the cheap chip route.

To make chip cards cost effective, banks will need to find ways of generating additional income from them by giving added value to holders. One way of doing this might be by creating a system where chip cards can be used for very low value transactions, even to buy a newspaper. A chip card could be developed which includes a "pre-payment" or 'stored value' section. This would allow cardholders to push the card into a terminal, to make a small purchase, which then deducts the money from the card's electronic purse. Not only might this be a useful feature for the customer but the pre-paid element would also provide a pool of money on which the bank could earn interest. The Mondex card may prove to be an example of such a card.

Risks of chip cards

As we have said, the motivation for moving towards the more expensive chip card over the older, cheaper magnetic stripe is its greater security.

106

When chip cards are introduced, there will be a move away from signature verification towards PINs. In this eventuality, the need for authorisation of transactions could decline. Because chip cards are less easy to fake, authorisation would be needed just for credit risk –is the holder over his limit? – rather than fraud risk – is the card a fake?

However, although chip cards may mean safer transactions, their development brings its own very substantial risks for the banks.

The biggest of these is the cost of developing the technology. It is reckoned that the banks will need to invest around £100m in the UK alone. However, they cannot avoid the risk that the system developed may become out-of-date rapidly, or that it is not as fraud proof as the banks had hoped – which would rapidly negate much of the reasoning for developing chip cards in the first place.

Telecommunications

Competition between BT and Mercury has already led to cheaper telephone calls in the UK. There is also likely to be competition from abroad, with US telecommunications companies already beginning to start operating in the UK market.

In tandem with this, VISA and MasterCard are putting pressure on UK telecom providers to reduce the cost of authorisation calls. As the cost of these calls falls, so the number of transactions that are authorised will be increased.

As well as verifying individual transactions, telecommunications have an important role to play in tackling fraud in other ways. A list of stolen cards can be transmitted direct to the merchants' terminals, which means they will automatically pick up a dubious card if it is presented. This gives a far higher detection rate than the old paper list, which relied on the merchant manually checking it.

ELEVEN

LAUNCHING A CREDIT CARD: THE CHECKLIST

In order to launch a credit card, there are a number of areas that need to be considered and key decisions that need to be made. Below, we provide a summary of these together with a checklist.

The market

If you are planning to enter a particular credit card market, you should be sure you know it extremely well. Experience and knowledge of a market in, say, one country is no guarantee of success in another.

For example, in 1988, Chase Manhattan introduced a low–interest VISA card in the UK. This card was launched on the basis of the success enjoyed by the bank with a similar product in the US. However, there were and are important differences between the two markets. In particular, in America the level of detailed credit information available means it is possible for companies to effectively pre–screen mailing lists. Before sending out mailshots in the US, Chase could be fairly sure that it would accept most subsequent applications. This means that companies do not waste money targeting customers they don't want. In the UK, however, there is no general access to this kind of "white" credit information (see Chapter Seven) and so companies are reduced to being less focused with their mailings. Clearly, this is likely to be a far less efficient, cost–effective method of promotion. It is thought to be one reason why Chase Manhattan's launch did not have the level of success in the UK that the bank might have liked.

Market research

As well as knowing the market, a company needs to be sure it can provide a product which that market actually wants. The proposed credit card is likely to need to have some kind of "unique selling point", or competitive advantage which sets it apart from other providers and which will be attractive to customers.

To test the strength of the proposed product, it will be necessary to conduct market research, both qualitative – to help refine and improve the original idea – and quantitative – to make sure enough people will want it. Quite clearly, there is no point in having a brilliant product, honed in every detail, if only a very few people will want it. Before proceeding with a launch, you need to be as certain as possible that there will be enough demand to make the product commercially viable.

Business rationale

There also needs to be a logical reason, from the company's perspective, for the launch. It may simply be to make additional profit by adding a new product line; it may be to give a more balanced portfolio of services; it may be to attract new customers in order to cross–sell existing services; it may be to increase market share. Whatever the reason for wanting to launch a credit card, it needs to fit logically into your wider business rationale.

Recruit personnel

If the launch will mean introducing the product into a new market, it is essential to hire the right calibre of staff. Probably the most crucial appointment is that of the individual who will head the organisation. It is essential that he or she has experience and expertise in the market. Such qualities will not, however, come cheaply.

When the UK building societies began entering the credit card market, many of them faced problems with hiring top staff. For historical reasons, building societies tended to pay chief executives lower salaries than those paid by the banks. When setting up their credit card arms, the salaries the building societies were prepared to pay for people to run them tended to be lower than the norm in the credit card sector. The result of this was that those from the banking industry who applied for these posts tended to be less experienced. The less experience, the greater the likelihood that wrong decisions will be taken and that things will go awry.

If you are planning to launch a credit card, you should be prepared to pay the price for getting the right person for the job. The salary involved will still be a relatively small proportion of the total operating costs.

The top individual needs to have the following qualities and experience:

- he or she needs knowledge of both marketing, and the operations and financial side of the credit card industry. In my experience, marketeers will often be quite capable of meeting sales targets, but pay too little attention to the profit and loss account. The ideal candidate will have strengths in both areas.

- the candidate will need to have general management experience. In a start–up situation, it is particularly important for him to be a good staff manager, demonstrating leadership and charisma. He will need drive and tenacity.

In reality, of course, it may not be possible to find this mix of qualities in a single candidate. This being the case, it is important that any areas of relative weakness are compensated for by the missing skills being apparent in his immediate team.

Whoever has overall responsibility needs to be senior enough to be trusted to get on with the job – although it is also important that his activities should be monitored.

Other key appointments to consider will be in the area of personnel, training, credit control, legal, finance and marketing (all of which are discussed in more detail below).

Location

If the operation is being set up from scratch, premises will need to be found. If you are running a credit card operation servicing the whole of the UK market, your operation needs to be fairly centrally based, ideally in a low–cost location.

Given the benefits of being central, it does raise the question of why Access should be based at Southend, and Trustcard in Brighton, both of which have the sea on one side. Could it be that the original chief executives of these organisations lived near these seaside locations?

The site chosen should also be near a pool of labour which is either experienced, or capable of being trained.

Security

Security is another major consideration. Your chosen premises will need to house vital material including new credit cards and confidential data. They should, therefore, be capable of being secured to the same degree that would be necessary if you were safeguarding cash.

Communications

Communications are another vital factor when choosing your location. Your operations will need to be well served by road, rail air and telecommunications.

For example, in the US, FDR, the credit card processing company, is located in the relatively out–of–the–way spot of Omaha. The reason for that is that Omaha was, at one time, the home of the US Strategic Air Command. The area, therefore, had excellent telecommunications links, on which FDR was able to capitalise.

Personnel and training

The credit card industry relies heavily on the use of technology, but it also needs considerable input from large numbers of human beings. Staff need to be properly paid, managed and trained. To do this, you will need competent personnel and training managers. In general, on the personnel side, experience in credit card operations may not be absolutely essential. However, as far as your training manager is concerned, he will need to have excellent technical knowledge which can be imparted very quickly, which is likely to be gained from previous, similar experience.

Processing of transactions

Transactions can either be handled in-house or subcontracted to a specialist processing company.

If you plan to operate in-house, you need to choose between building a bespoke computer system from scratch, or buying an existing package. The latter may seem the cheaper option. However, in practice, if you buy a package you are likely to need to make amendments to tailor it for your particular needs. If the changes are extensive, it may prove almost as expensive as starting from scratch. On the other hand, if you are planning to create your own system, you will need to be sure that you have the necessary expertise available.

One advantage of transaction being processed in-house – whether on a bespoke or off–the–shelf system – is that you can achieve economies of scale. You may have the fairly high fixed costs of setting up the system, but once you are up and running, the costs are relatively low. Additional transactions can be put through the system at a very low marginal cost.

If you are planning to subcontract your processing, in the UK, there are two main options available: using FDR (part of the US conglomerate which processes over half of the total transactions in the US), or the Bank of Scotland, which runs a similar processing operation.

The disadvantage of going outside is that you cannot achieve economies of scale. In general, these companies charge per transaction – so the more you put through, the more you pay. It may, of course, be possible to negotiate pricing agreements which reflect economies of scale.

With subcontracting, you will also have less control over system enhancements which may take time to be developed and implemented. If you are handling your own processing, you may be able to rush through a system development eg. in response to changes by a competitor.

Card production

At the centre of your planning should be the card itself (see below for card design). The card will need to be embossed and encoded, and, again, you have the choice of doing this yourself or subcontracting to a bureau, such as National Business Systems (NBS) in Byfleet.

This decision will generally be a function of the numbers: if you are going to be issuing more than half a million cards a year, it is likely to become cost effective to buy the equipment to do it yourself. If not, subcontracting may be your best option.

Marketing strategy

If your marketing is to be successful, you need to hire the right marking professional. He or she does not necessarily need to have previous credit card experience, although this may be useful.

You need to decide whether you are competing on price, or on some other factor. For example, Save & Prosper competes on the basis of having a lower interest rate; Barclaycard operates on non–price competition, with profile points and other benefits; MBNA appears to compete successfully with a mix of price competition and client service.

Another important aspect of marketing is the design of the card literature. If you can attach some prestige to the card by the design of its promotional material, you may be able to attract a segment of your potential market you might otherwise have missed.

Distribution

How are you going to sell the card? There are several options: advertising, public relations, direct mail, co–branding, affinity cards. There is no single approach which is right all the time. Your best option will depend what type of organisation you are. If you are, say, NatWest with a substantial branch network, rather than spend money on advertising to recruit new cardholders, you could train and target your branch staff to sell to existing customers.

Building card usage

Marketing the card to encourage people to apply is one thing, encouraging them to use it once they have it is another. This is a task which will normally be done by advertising, direct mail and sales promotion.

Card design

The design of the card itself is also crucial – and reasonably time–consuming. You should allow at least three to four months from seeing the artists' impression of the card through to production of the finished plastic. If you are planning to carry the VISA or MasterCard logo (see below), each stage of the design will need to be approved by the relevant organisation.

International links

If you want your card to be generally acceptable by merchants, you will need to join either VISA or MasterCard and sport the appropriate logo. This involves seeking approval from the chosen organisation. Applicants need to submit a business plan to these organisations for approval. You should allow a minimum of four months, and even up to eight months, for your application to be approved. Because of the time involved, this is a consideration to put in hand very early in the process, ideally at the same time as you are choosing your location (see above).

Credit assessment

An experienced credit controller may be essential but, again, the right person may not come cheaply.

There are two options for credit assessment: by credit scoring (see Chapter Seven), or on a judgmental basis.

As we discussed earlier, credit scoring will be more objective than a judgmental approach. However, if you are starting out, you will not have your own data on which to base your allocation of credit points and you will need initially to rely on score cards developed from the experience of other banks.

If you plan to use credit scoring and are starting from scratch, you can buy in expertise from credit scoring consultants, such as Fair Isaacs or CCN.

You will also need to establish on–line links with a credit reference agency. This means that, when a customer applies, you can automatically check whether he has any "black" information recorded against him (see Chapter Seven). Hopefully in due course "white information" will become the norm! These links may take up to three months to establish, so, again, it is important to get this process underway early.

Legal

A credit card operation has to comply with the panoply of legislation outlined in Chapter Nine.

You will also need to draw up a range of standard contracts, including cardholder agreements and merchant agreements. This may be done, either by recruiting staff expertise in consumer credit, or buying in legal advice from a firm of solicitors.

In one bank's experience, going to a large London firm of solicitors was not cost effective. The firm used to draft the agreements contrived to leave out a vital clause, which was subsequently picked up by a fairly junior member of the bank's staff who had experience of the Consumer Credit Act. In this instance, the bank had to scrap much of the material it had already had printed.

Technology

Cards can operate using two broad types of technology: magnetic stripes and chip cards. In broad terms, companies should try to follow industry trends, rather than attempt to lead. Taking a lead in technology could prove inordinately expensive if you make the wrong decision. The most prudent course may be to keep a watchful eye on developments in the US (on the basis that what happens there, subsequently happens here), while maintaining close links with industry bodies in the UK, such as the Card Payments Group which meets under the auspices of APACS.

Finance and financial modelling

You will need to recruit a senior staff member with sound finance experience, although not necessarily gained in the credit card industry. Experience of financial controls and financial modelling is, however, essential. He should also be in sympathy with the marketing and selling side of the operation. Someone who views, say, an advertising campaign merely as a cost, rather than as an investment for obtaining more business in future, is not likely to be a wise appointment.

When assessing the financial viability of a new credit card operation, I believe you should aim to recover the direct costs of obtaining new business within two to three years of putting that business on the books. Ideally, you should aim for a fairly short pay–back period, although in some circumstances, this may have to extend up to five years.

Whoever is funding the operation must be happy with the proposed timescale. During the first two or three years of a new card operation, the losses are likely to be quite large and it is important that the sponsors are prepared to keep their faith with what is being done. The sponsor needs to understand that, although losses are incurred during the initial years, when the profits start to come in, they are likely to be substantial.

The Financial Controller should be able to create financial models, which allow you to put "what if?" questions. For example, *what* would be the impact on the profit and loss account *if* we cut the interest rate by x per cent?

CHECKLIST:

- assess the potential market. Is it viable commercially?

- recruit appropriate personnel. Do not expect the necessary experience and expertise to come cheaply;

- decide your marketing strategy;

- organise your staff training programme;

- choose your location;

- decide on international links. Be prepared to wait four to eight months for approval from the relevant organisation;

- allow at least four months to design and approve the design of the card itself;

- decide on the appropriate technology to adopt;

- decide whether to process transactions in or out house;

- decide whether to encode or emboss the cards in-house or outside;

- decide whether to use credit scoring or a judgmental approach;

- decide debt collection procedures;

- decide on your financial controls;

- put the legal aspects, agreements, contracts etc., in hand.

TWELVE

THE FUTURE

Future developments in the credit card market are not clear cut. Not surprisingly, the further you look into the future, the harder it becomes to predict what will happen. However, there are a number of likely developments affecting both the UK and the rest of Europe.

UK MARKET

The credit card market in the UK is already fairly well saturated. We are unlikely, therefore, to see an increase in its size in absolute terms. However, there will still be changes within it – as older customers die and are replaced by new and younger people.

Market segmentation

Although the overall size of the market is set to remain relatively static, it is likely to be divided up in different ways. Customers are already split into those who take extended credit (and so pay interest) and the so-called free riders – those who always pay off their debt each month and so avoid interest charges.

Companies are likely to develop products which are aimed specifically at one group or the other. The banks may well continue in their attempts to move free riders away from credit cards and towards debit cards. This will involve continuing charging an annual fee for credit cards, while providing debit cards free of charge. In this way, the banks would hope to end up with a credit card customer base of all credit takers.

Another possible area of segmentation could be by credit risk. Those customers who are deemed a poorer risk than others could be charged a higher rate of interest. Again, this is already happening to some extent. Providers like Save & Prosper are already offering more competitive rates of interest to customers, on the basis that it will accept only those individuals with a good credit rating. If the bigger banks are not to lose their customers who are the best credit risk to competitors like Save & Prosper, they may start developing different tiers of interest for different cardholders. This kind of approach would allow them to keep the rates charged to those with the best credit rating at a competitive level.

There is already a precedent for this type of differentiation between customers according to risk. In the 1970s, most motor insurers operated on a tariff basis. Whichever company you contacted would be likely to quote you the same premium rate for providing cover. However, as new firms began entering the market, they started offering discounted prices to those drivers who were deemed to be a lower risk.

In the credit card market at the present time, customers are not particularly price sensitive. In general, they may moan at the rates of interest being charged, but they do not shop around for a better deal. Most people who have, say, an account with Midland Bank will also have a Midland credit card, despite the fact that there is nothing to stop them having one from, say, Barclays if it offers a better deal. However, credit card customers are only likely to become more price sensitive as time goes on and once they start voting with their feet in significant numbers, the banks will almost inevitably respond by changes to their products.

Non-price competition

There is also likely to be scope for greater non-price competition. Some card issuers will hope to use increasingly other means of differentiating their products to get and retain customers. This would include incentives such as Air Miles and Profile points, offering free personal injury insurance, or cover for goods bought with the credit card, or by enhancing the service provided to the customer in some other way.

In the US, the National Bank of Maryland (MBNA) has already built up a substantial card operation primarily on the basis of its customer service. It has now set up in the UK, where it is set to try to duplicate its American success. In the main, it will tend to be the larger credit card companies which will be placing greater emphasis on non-price competition.

New players

The old stalwarts of the UK market are likely to find themselves facing competition from a host of new players, many of whom may be foreign-based companies.

We have already discussed MBNA (see above), which is soon to be joined by another US bank, Citibank. American banks are especially likely to be eyeing the UK as their own home market is highly competitive and the scope for increasing profit potential, therefore, somewhat limited. These American operators are beginning to look increasingly at developing operations in the UK and Europe.

But while the UK's home-grown operators can expect to find themselves competing with American companies, they are less likely to face competition from European banks. This is partly because of the language barrier, which inevitably makes setting up in a new jurisdiction more problematic, and partly because credit cards have not taken off to any great extent in much of Europe, where debit cards hold greater sway.

Another factor is that the UK market is already more competitive than much of Europe. Traditionally, companies in the most competitive areas move into regions of less competition (hence the interest in the UK of US firms). Therefore, banks in Europe are likely to be rather hesitant about entering the UK market.

Chip cards

Chip or integrated circuit cards are an almost inevitable development (see Chapter Seven). Testing of their use is expected to start in the UK within the next couple of years. Although chip cards are considerably more expensive than traditional magnetic stripe cards, they are much less susceptible to fraud and will, therefore, be likely to be attractive to card issuers. As we said earlier in Chapter Seven, **chip cards are likely to be widely used by the end of the decade.**

Secured card facilities

Secured card facilities are already a feature in the US. Where an individual has a poor credit record and would not otherwise qualify for a credit card, he or she may be offered a secured card instead. This would mean the cardholder depositing money with the bank, which stands as security against goods and services paid for with the card.

Alternatively, the customer would deposit, say, his portfolio of shares with the bank which would be security for sums loaned on the card. In return for the security, the customer would be offered an especially low rate of interest – perhaps 2.5 per cent above base rate. Such a client would need, of course, to have a good credit record.

EUROPE

The advent of the Single Market may not, in fact, lead to any large scale cross-border issuing of cards. There are a number of reasons why this may be the case, some of which may be cultural (which we look at below), while others are to do with regulation.

Despite the Single Market, the central banks in each jurisdiction are still able to impose regulations which can make it very difficult for a bank from another country to start marketing its products within that area. We have already seen an example of this when Barclays attempted to launch its interest-bearing account in France. The Banque of France was able to effectively prevent Barclays from doing so by imposing local restrictions on this type of account. It is believed that the Banque of France was concerned that the competition from Barclays might mean reduced profits for its domestic banks. Reduced profits could lead to more banking failures and correspondingly make the job of regulation more difficult.

The different cultures and banking traditions in each European country are also likely to act against cross-border issuing. In France, debit cards are much more popular than credit cards. In Germany, the most prevalent payment method is the eurocheque, with plastic cards taking off only extremely slowly.

Payment organisations in Europe

VISA is likely to restructure its European, Middle Eastern and African Region (see Chapter Three) so that Africa and the Middle East are segmented into a new region. It also seems probable that the developing countries of Eastern Europe will similarly be divided, so that VISA can concentrate on Continental Europe and the UK in order to try to head off competition from Europay.

Telecom harmonisation

Credit card companies may wish to see the development of a uniform European-wide telecommunications system, which would facilitate cross-border marketing.

European Union legislation

Like every other field of commerce, credit cards are set to be affected by legislation emanating from the European Union (EU). Proposed EU Directives on unfair contract terms are likely to mean that card issuers will have to revise their agreements with their customers. It should be remembered the proposed EU Directives need to be adopted by the EU and then included in UK legislation. Unilaterally changing the rate of interest is likely to be ruled out. Instead, card issuers will need to lay down exactly what steps they will follow and how any increase will be communicated to their customers.

The proposed law on unfair contracts will mean that credit card agreements will be subject to scrutiny; where a clause is deemed unreasonable, it will be treated as void. This will not, however, mean the whole contract being declared void. For example, where there is a disputed transaction, the bank may state that it refuses to intervene between the cardholder and the retailer. This might be regarded as unfair and, therefore, void – but the contract as a whole will not necessarily be void.

Claims under Section 75 of the Consumer Credit Act (see Chapter Eight) may also be affected by EU regulations. The duty imposed by UK domestic law on credit card issuers to compensate customers for faulty or non-delivery of goods is more onerous than that provided for under European legislation. In Europe, the card issuer is the "insurer" of last resort only whereas under UK legislation, the customer has an equal right to seek compensation from the card issuer or from the merchant. This, then, is one area of European law which will work in favour of UK credit card issuers.

EU law will also have an impact on distance selling. It sets down procedures that must be followed if selling by telephone or remotely in some other way. If the rules are not followed, the transaction may be declared void and the credit card issuer would have to reimburse the cost to the cardholder.

Card issuers will also face changes to the way they charge for cross border transactions. At the present time, card issuers do not have to spell this out; they often merely state that the bank will determine the exchange rate used. Most of them currently add around 2-2.75 per cent to the inter–bank exchange rate. Under the EU regulations, however, card issuers will be required to set out clearly their charging structure and this is likely to have to be linked to some internationally acceptable rate of exchange, perhaps 2 per cent above the prevailing inter–bank rate of exchange. Any other charges would also have to be spelled out to the cardholder.

Retailer groups

Retailer groups already have a strong record of pressuring credit card companies in the UK to make changes in their favour. These groups have also developed a strong voice within the EU and it seems likely, therefore, that this is a trend which is likely to continue.

Overall

There is likely to be greater competition among card issuers and merchant acquirers. Customers are likely to become more financially aware and, therefore, demanding. If their demands are not satisfied fully, they will be more likely than at present to change their cards.

APPENDIX ONE:

A GLOSSARY OF TERMS

Access
The credit card scheme originally launched in October 1972 by Lloyds, Midland, NatWest and The Royal Bank of Scotland and now linked to Europay/MasterCard.

Affinity card
A bank issued card linked to a particular group of people or organisation.

Amex
American Express, who operate a worldwide charge card scheme.

Authorisation
The agreement of a card issuer to a specific transaction by a merchant via a credit card. An authorisation code is notified by telephone or telex to the merchant who records it on the sales voucher. (see also **Floor limit**).

Automated Teller Machine (ATM)
An ATM is a computerised self–service device enabling the cardholder of an appropriate card to withdraw cash from either a bank or credit card account and access to other services. Earlier versions were called cash dispensers.

Barclaycard
A credit card launched by Barclays Bank in 1966 and a founder member of VISA International. (see also **Access**)

Cardholder
The individual to whom a card has been issued.

Card Issuer
The bank, building society or retailer which issues cards to customers.

Cash card
A card issued by a financial institution enabling the holder to use an ATM. See ATM card.

Card Dispenser
See ATM.

Charge card
A payment card where the cardholder is required to settle the outstanding balance in full at the end of a short period (usually a month). The majority of Gold cards operate as charge cards.

Cheque guarantee card
A card issued by a financial institution which guarantees the payment of cheques drawn by the cardholder up to a defined limit.

Chip card
See Integrated Circuit Card

Co–branded card
A card promoted jointly by a bank and another, non–financial, institution.

Company card
A card (usually a charge card) issued to a business for use by the directors or employees to pay for business expenditure.

Credit card
An instrument of payment which enables the cardholder to obtain either goods or services from merchants where arrangements have been made (directly or indirectly) by the card issuer, who also makes arrangements to reimburse the merchant. The cardholder settles with the card issuer in accordance with the terms of the particular scheme. In certain instances credit cards may be used to obtain cash either from bank and building society branches or from ATMs.

Credit scoring
A method of credit appraisal used by most credit card companies to vet applications for credit facilities.

Debit card
A payment card used to obtain cash, goods and services automatically debiting the payments to the cardholders' bank or building society account. It is usually combined with other functions such as ATM operation and cheque guarantee.

Diners' Club
A worldwide charge card scheme.

Europay International SA
The European business partner of MasterCard. It was created out of the merger of Eurocard and eurocheque.

Extended credit/Revolving credit
A facility offered by bank credit cards and some store cards whereby the cardholder may elect to repay only a proportion of the amount owing.

Floor limit
The maximum value of transaction which a merchant may accept without obtaining authorisation from the card issuer.

Fuel card
A retailer card usually restricted to the purchase of petrol, oil and accessories.

Gold card
A card aimed at the card issuers more affluent customers.

In–house card
A retailer card for use at the establishments of that retailer only. (see **Store card**).

Integrated Circuit Card
Known as a 'chip' card, it holds personal information about the cardholder and can be used in conjuction with a PIN.

JCB card
A card issued by the Japan Credit Bureau.

Magnetic stripe
A technical device by which pre–recorded information is stored on a **payment** card.

MasterCard International Inc.
A bank–owned payment organisation which facilitates the exchange and settlement of transactions. It is the business partner of Europay International SA in Europe.

Merchant
A supplier of goods or services.

Merchant agreement
The contractual terms between the merchant acquiring bank and the merchant.

Merchant service charge
The charge made to merchants by merchant acquiring banks on the value of transactions made by payment cards.

Merchant outlet
A merchant's place of trading.

Mondex card
A prepayment card. (see Chapter One).

Multi-function card
A card which fulfils two or more functions eg. credit and cheque guarantee.

Option card
Usually a retailer card offering extended credit as well as the option of settling within a month.

Payment card
A generic word meaning all credit, debit and any other similar type of payment card.

PIN
Personal identification number. Known only to the cardholder, who uses it for identification normally to obtain access to ATM.

Petrol card
See **Fuel card**.

POS
Point of sale.

Private label card
A card operated by a financial institution for use by the customers of an individual merchant.

Retailer
See **Merchant.**

Retailer card
A credit card issued by merchants (often the large retail stores) to encourage sales at their outlets. (see **Store card**).

Sales voucher
A document completed by the merchant in respect of goods and services provided for the cardholder (who signs it).

Smart card
See **Integrated Circuit Card.**

Store card
Usually a two–party card issued by a retail store.

Switch
An electronic debit card scheme which enables holders of Switch cards to make payments at merchants accepting Switch cards. The payments are charged directly to the retailer's bank account from the cardholder's bank account.

Supplier
See **Merchant.**

Telephone card
This is either a pre–payment card or BT's credit card.

Trader
See **Merchant.**

Travel & entertainment card
Usually known as a T and E card. (see **Charge card**) eg. Amex and Diner's.

VISA International Service Association
A bank–owned payment organisation which facilitates the exchange and settlement of transactions.

APPENDIX TWO:

A BRIEF HISTORY OF CREDIT CARDS

Credit cards in their modern form first developed in the United States at the start of this century. The first was issued in 1914. General Petroleum Corporation of California (now Mobil Oil) supplied cards to employees and selected customers. In 1915, coins or tokens (called 'shoppers plates') were issued by a number of small hotels and stores, telegraph companies and railroads, and, in effect, provided the customer with a monthly credit account. There was no provision for extended credit. Reciprocal arrangements between establishments followed. The petrol companies attempted to stimulate sales by the issuing of proprietary cards.

In 1950, Diners' Club was incorporated. It was the brainchild of two business associates, Frank McNamara and Ralph Schneider, who came to the end of a restaurant meal with friends and discovered they did not have cash to pay the bill. It was therefore arranged for their friends and business colleagues to pay their hotel and restaurant accounts in New York on a monthly account basis on production of their Diners' Club card. No limits were placed on the amount of credit except that accounts were settled at the end of the month and there was no extended credit provided. Members also received a directory of establishments where the card would be accepted. This was the start of the development of 'T' and 'E' cards (standing for travel and entertainment) and was soon followed by American Express and Carte Blanche.

Three years earlier, in 1947, the Flatbush National Bank in New York had introduced its 'Charge–it' plan, a monthly charge account confined to customers of the bank. In August 1951, the Franklin National Bank became the first bank to issue credit cards to customers of other banks and bankers saw an opportunity to provide consumer credit. By 1957, 26 banks had 754,000 cardholders being accepted by 11,000 merchants; turnover exceeded US$40 million. In reality however, this represented slow growth as a consequence of the difficulties the banks were facing, probably high setting up and running costs, frauds and the reluctance of merchants to pay a discount on sales. On the East Coast, Chase Manhattan sold off its credit card department in 1962 partly as a result of the structure of the

Federal banking system which restricted branch networks to the home territory and made the interstate acceptance of credit cards by merchants difficult to organise. In 1965, Pittsburgh National Bank and the Mellon National Bank introduced their own card programmes.

BankAmericard

In California, however, a different picture was emerging. In 1959, the Bank of America entered the bank card field and quickly expanded operations through its extensive West Coast branch network which meant that its card was acceptable throughout the State. Initially running costs were high: customer's sales slips were sorted manually and returned with monthly accounts. There was even some consideration given to terminating the entire operation. However by 1961, BankAmericard had achieved one million cardholders (T/O $75 million) and by 1967 this had increased to 2.7 million cardholders (T/O $335 million). In 1966, the Bank of America set up BankAmericard Service Corporation which undertook the licensing of its schemes for a fee to other banks: the Corporation maintained a tight control over the issuing of its cards. The scheme was successful because bankers avoided the complexities of starting their own programmes and cardholders found they could use their BankAmericard when they travelled to other States. By 1970, 3,301 banks were affiliated to the scheme.

MasterCard

The major Californian banks quickly became aware of the competitive threat from BankAmericard and so Wells Fargo Bank, United California Bank, Bank of California and Crocker National Bank formed the California Bank Card Association as a non–profit organisation issuing a common bank credit card. The Association then purchased the rights to use the 'Master Charge' name and card design from the First National Bank of Louisville, Kentucky. A jointly–funded computer centre was established and the operation soon achieved profitability.

In other parts of the USA, credit card plans were developing and in those States which allowed branch banking, large banks offered a statewide service. Such banks included Marine Midland Bank in New York and Valley National Bank in Arizona. In States which did not allow branch banking, a number of regional associations were formed. Many of the major banks in Chicago formed the Midwest Bankcard Association to provide credit cards for the Illinois and Indiana markets.

In 1967 seven bank card schemes jointly established the Interbank Card Association to allow interchange between different regions of the country. Local identities were maintained and the Association (and the right to interchange) was indicated by a small white 'i' within a black circle appearing in the lower right–hand corner of the card. Merchants however were unfamiliar with the design and its lack of acceptability posed difficulties.

In 1969, the California Bank Card Association (now known as the Western States Bankcard Association) conveyed all of its rights in the 'Master Charge' logo and service marks to the Inter-bank Card Association. Members of Interbank started reissuing their cards showing the 'Master Charge' logo and new bank card centres were licensed. The South East Bankers Association in Atlanta and the Mountain States Bankcard Association in Denver joined Interbank.

By 1970, almost every state in the USA was represented by banks promoting either 'Master Charge' or 'BankAmericard'.

International developments

The American Express Company introduced the American Express card in 1958 as a 'T and E' card. An immediate need arose for USA cardholders travelling abroad in Europe on business and holidays to use their cards. The first sterling card was issued in 1963 and in 1966 a regional headquarters (covering Europe, the Middle East and Africa) was established in the UK.

In 1966, the BankAmerica Service Corporation allowed Barclays Bank to use the colours of BankAmericard. In 1970, the Bank of America sold off the BankAmerica Service Corporation which became the independent National BankAmericard Incorporated (NBI). In 1974, a separate international organisation, IBANCO, was formed. The terms of the contract included the name 'Bank-Americard' reverting to the Bank of America in 1979. This coincided with a need to make the card better known internationally: the word 'VISA' was selected because of its universal acceptance and understanding and in 1977 NBI became VISA USA and IBANCO became VISA International. In 1979 Interbank announced a change of name and card design. By 1983, the change from Master Charge to MasterCard was completed.

From its inception National BankAmericard prohibited members from participating in any other national card system. This was tested in the Courts by the Worthan Bank in Little Rock, Arkansas, in a legal battle lasting six years. Eventually this was settled in 1976 when the by–law of the National BankAmericard was declared discriminatory and was thus removed. Initially duality confused bank customers particularly as it coincided with the change from BankAmericard to VISA, but it soon became accepted for MasterCard and VISA to be seen together worldwide.

The United States: domestic expansion

The subsequent development of bank–issued credit cards has been dominated by the evolution of the two national systems provided by MasterCard and VISA. Much of their success has been due to the results achieved for their members by the development of nationwide advertising programmes using contemporary media methods. Detailed regulations governing the operations of the individual schemes cover the use of logos and servicemarks, and specifications, authorisation rules, floor limits, restricted card lists, merchant relationships, cash advances, settlement and interchange, charge banks, security and fraud, and counterfeiting.

One of the key areas has been authorisation with the early system of telephone or telex confirmation becoming unworkable as volume increased. Computerised networks were developed: MasterCard's INAS (Interbank National Authorisation System) and BASE –1.

Two computer networks were also established for interchange (the clearing of credit card transactions): MasterCard's INET (Interbank Network for Electronic Transfer) and VISA's BASE–11. Both systems require that its members send and receive interchange electronically. Sales slips are only forwarded to the home bank if the document is illegible or in the event of charge back (when a merchant's account is debited because of a specific problem). A portion of the merchant service charge is paid to the card issuing bank as an interchange fee.

When member banks cannot agree over rules, both Interbank and VISA implement a grievance procedure: penalties are charged to the losing bank.

Rules and regulations

There has also been much change in the legal and regulatory environment in the United States affecting the operations of the banks issuing credit cards. Before 1968, Congress left the regulation of consumer credit to the individual States. However, in that year the first parts of the Consumer Credit Protection Act were passed, including the Truth in Lending Act requiring a meaningful disclosure of important credit terms. The impending regulation, Regulation Z issued by the Federal Reserve Board, imposed detailed rules and substantial penalties for non–compliance. The Act also covered the advertising of credit terms.

In 1970, Congress amended the Act to prohibit the unsolicited distribution of credit cards and to limit each customer's liability for unauthorised use of a lost or stolen card to $50 and even then subject to certain conditions. However, public concern over the complexity of the Act and Regulation Z led to the 1980 Truth in Lending Simplification and Reform Act (effective in April 1982).

The Fair Credit Reporting Act 1971 restricted the purposes for which credit bureaux could give out information and was an early indication of concern over personal information. The Privacy Act 1974 regulated the activities of federal agencies in collecting information on individuals and established the Privacy Protection Study Commission. Their report 'Personal Privacy in an Informed Society' published in 1977 ultimately led to the Privacy Act 1978 which generally forbade financial institutions from disclosing a customers' records to government officials without the customer's written agreement or a written legal demand.

The Fair Credit Billing Act 1974 established consumer's rights on alleged accounting errors and allowed cardholders in certain circumstances to withhold payment for damaged or poor–quality goods and services. The Act also prohibits merchants from offering discounts to encourage buyers to pay by cash or cheques instead of credit card. The Equal Credit Opportunity Act 1974 (implemented by Regulation B) prohibited discrimination based on sex, marriage, age, race, colour, religion or being in receipt of public assistance benefits.

The Fair Debt Collection Practices Act 1977 regulated debt collection practices and the Electronic Fund Transfer Act 1978 (implemented by Regulation E) established rules for the unsolicited distribution of EFT cards, customer's liability for unauthorised transactions and many of the other rules for credit cards contained in the Truth in Lending Act.

The introduction and development of debit cards

When banks world–wide sought to expand use of electronic funds transfer (EFT) through point of sale terminals (POS), automated teller machines (ATM) to produce income sufficient to justify the capital investment necessary, they chose to allow entry by means of plastic cards. However, had they restricted the service to their credit cardholders they would have limited the service and excluded individuals who did not qualify for credit. They therefore introduced the debit card. Debit cards did not involve extended credit, but they did allow access to EFT technology.

One of the first organisations to issue a debit card was the First Federal Savings and Loan Association of Lincoln, Nebraska, through its wholly owned subsidiary TMS Corporation of the Americas. The Federal Home Loan Bank Board approved the introduction of 'The Money Service' (TMS) in 1968. Six years later TMS was established in two Hinky Dinky supermarkets enabling customers to use their debit cards for cash withdrawals or deposits. By 1976 TMS had expanded to 17 bank branches in 10 cities and 42 retail locations. Both the State of Nebraska and the Nebraskan Independent Bankers Association brought suits against First Federal for violation of state banking laws.

Neither succeeded and this encouraged a number of financial institutions to introduce similar debit card operations. The Californian Federal Savings and Loan Association quickly entered this market, and the combined department and food store Fred Meyer Inc. in Oregon, through its subsidiary Fred Meyer Savings and Loans. This organisation introduced mini branches near the checkout counters for various types of deposits, withdrawals and cheque cashing services together with on–line direct terminals for credit transmissions to the merchants' accounts and debits to customers' accounts. By early 1976 the Federal Home Loan Bank Board had approved 54 applications involving the use of the plastic card.

Simultaneously, the commercial banks were developing their use of proprietary debit cards in order to increase the utilisation of their ATM's. By 1975 25% of commercial banks had ATM's (there were 4,500 machines in use) and 12% were offering the service of debit cards. In New York, Citibank were developing 'Citicard', an on–line terminal network and within a year over one million cards had been issued. At the merchant location, the Citicard acted as a cheque guarantee card. In October 1975 Citicard 11 was introduced (later renamed 'Transaction'), which extended the service to account holders at other banks.

Most of the other large commercial banks began to develop their own systems. Wells Fargo Bank introduced 'WellService'. Some services were franchised and other banks formed themselves into regional associations, such as Financial Communication Services Incorporated (FCS), involving banks in Missouri, Kansas, Iowa, Southern Illinois and Western Kentucky. FCS provided participating banks with services such as card manufacture, installation and maintenance of terminals, cardholders' authorisation, switching, data input and batch transmissions, personal identification number (PIN) issuance, interbank settlement and reconciliation.

The two national card companies also entered the debit card market and in August 1975 NBI introduced the 'Entree' card with the authorisation network being established on BASE–I (used for BankAmericard). Interchange for out of area transactions was made via the BASE–II electronic network.

In response, Interbank Card Association developed 'Signet' which initially was marketed as a cheque guarantee card, although it was to provide a nation-wide debit card facility for further development.

The bank card phenomenon

Following in the wake of the successful bank credit cards came a series of developments as the American banking industry tried to provide practical methods of delivering financial services suited to the changing way of life. These needed to recognise the shift from city residency locality (ie. customers find it more difficult to visit city based branches outside office hours), increasing affluence and the involvement of women in financial matters.

Initially, in the mid–1960s, the credit card acted as a cheque guarantee card although difficulties occurred because of merchant reluctance to accept the cards. On–line systems evolved whereby validation of the credit card was made via the merchant's terminal. These schemes also proved to provide a low return on investment.

During the 1970s, point–of–sale services developed with high technological processing systems providing multi–services – credit card authorisation, cheque verification and authorisation and management information services.

The next major innovation was the ambiguously labelled debit card which fell into two main categories: proprietary cards issued by individual financial institutions and those issued by banks licensed by Interbank or VISA. The main value of debit cards was to allow on–line entry to current and deposit accounts particularly through the automated teller machines (ATM's).

In their book *Bank Cards,* the American Bankers Association said 'since the end of World War II, there has been an ever–increasing trend towards mass consumption and self–service operations. The bank credit card typifies the mass appeal and consumption of a specific financial service. The credit card is a form of self–service loan, to the degree that cardholders can make loans to themselves by using their cards for purchase and/or cash advances'.

ATM's have been a vital factor in the move towards self–service banking not only because they provide the customer with the ability to overcome inflexible banking hours but because they are a counter to the rising salary costs faced by the banks. 'ATM programmes will be the single most important service offered in this decade.'

Self–service banking may also mean that the place where the financial transaction is initiated moves from work locations (ATM's, banks) and the point–of–sale (the merchant) to the logical starting point, the customer's home, particularly as a result of the development of home computers. This was the scenario in the United States as the credit card matured into the last two decades of the twentieth century.

The United Kingdom

Joshua Kelly Waddilove was born in Bradford in 1840. He was 'an abstemious, pious man...with a genuine horror of the social abuses of the Victorian age. He believed the problems (such as common drunkenness) could be overcome through thrift and self help'. When 40, he began to issue 'cheques' to needy mothers at a weekly cost of a few pence. The cheques were redeemable by special arrangement with a local shop. The system proved popular, Waddilove opened his first office in Bradford and the Provident and Clothing Supply Company became a pioneer of the provision of consumer credit through the issuing of cheques and vouchers in the United Kingdom. D G Hanson wrote: 'It was the forerunner of credit cards in two respects, in that payment was made by a voucher and the customer enjoyed the benefit of revolving credit.'

In the early 1950s the Finders Dining Club Limited established reciprocal arrangements with Diners' Club Inc. in America. In 1954, it became Finders Services Limited and in 1962 it acquired the goodwill of Credit Card Facilities Club Limited and changed its name to the Diners Club Limited (known as Diners' Club). Two years later, Westminster Bank acquired 49.7% of the share equity and Diners' Club Inc just over 50%. In 1967 Lloyds and Martins Banks began to promote American Express cards. Together with Carte Blanche, whose UK office (established in 1966) was formed to develop a trader base for US visiting cardholders, American Express and Diners' Club ensured the expansion of charge cards in the United Kingdom.

Well aware of American card developments, British banks remained cautious although in October 1965, National Provincial introduced the cheque guarantee card which, subject to certain conditions, guaranteed the payment of the holders' cheques to a maximum value of £30. A few months later, the Midland Bank issued its own cheque cards to be followed by the majority of English, Scottish and Irish Banks.

Barclaycard

Barclays Bank became the first bank outside the United States to use the blue, white and gold coloured bands of BankAmericard: it also obtained the computer programme.

On 10 January 1966 the launch of Barclaycard was announced. The headquarters were at Northampton with processing centres subsequently established elsewhere including Liverpool, Kirkby, Birmingham, Stockton, Middlesborough, Leeds and Manchester. At its inception, the Barclaycard guaranteed cheques presented by Barclays Bank customers for cash at its branches: this was extended to the British Linen Bank (a Scottish clearing bank now owned by Bank of Scotland) and in 1968 to all cardholders (some of whom were not Barclays' account holders).

Although Barclaycard was the first multi–purpose card in the UK, it was as a credit card that it was to develop. The initial target was to recruit 1 million cardholders and 30,000 trade outlets. The early target proved difficult to achieve but by 1970 1.3 million cards had been issued. By 1979, this had increased to 4.9 million and by 1990 the number had reached around 8 to 9 million.

In 1977 when IBANCO changed its name to VISA International, Barclaycard began to use the VISA logo and the international popularity of credit cards continued to grow. Barclaycard was helped by five participant banks (one of the classes of membership of VISA International) which act as sponsored agents to recruit cardholders and sign up traders. Yorkshire Bank (32% owned by Barclays) and Bank of Scotland (35% owned by Barclays) continue to operate in this way but the Allied Irish Banks became a full member of VISA International in 1979 and took over Barclaycard operations in the Irish Republic. The Co–operative Bank and the Trustee Savings Banks (Barclaycard recruited the East Anglia Trustee Savings Bank in 1973) also decided to operate their own VISA cards.

Access
By 1970, National Westminster, Midland and Lloyds Banks realised that their individual cheque guarantee cards were not likely to withstand the competition from the Barclays' credit card. They were also worried by the situation whereby their customers were being recruited by Barclaycard. At the end of that year a joint Working Group was established as a consequence of which the three banks (later joined by Williams and Glyn's Bank and The Royal Bank of Scotland) formed the Joint Credit Card Company Limited. Although a full integration between the banks was rejected, a partial joint venture was set up to provide research and operational advice, marketing, promotion and advertising, data processing and accounting. Each bank retained independence for issuing cards and deciding credit limits. The decision to operate a joint venture was influenced partly by the resistance of retailers to the idea of too many stickers on shop doors.

The location selected for Access was Southend–on–Sea. By May 1972, 50,000 sales outlets had joined the scheme and Access was underway. By 1979 over 4 million cards had been issued.

The economic situation affected the growth of Access although turnover increased from £136 million in 1973 to £973 million in 1979. Cards issued increased from 3.2 million in 1975 to 4.05 million in 1979.

Faced with the need to match the international acceptability of Barclaycard, Access tried to join Interbank but negotiations floundered on the problem of reciprocal arrangements because Access did not have the data processing capability. For a time it joined the Eurocard System (explained below) but agreement was reached in June 1974 and in April 1975 Access became part of Interbank (later MasterCard).

The great strength of Access lay in the joint working of the administration. There were several large installations in Southend coping with the full range of advertising, issuing of cards (to the instructions of the individual banks), computation and despatch of statements, processing debit vouchers and cash and credit vouchers, and dealing with authorisations to retailers.

The economies of working together on such a scale are impressive but there were signs of frustration caused by the longer chain of command resulting from joint decision making. Security was much in evidence everywhere at Southend and no one bank could find out information about another bank's customers. The individual banks retained full control of setting interest rates for their customers, fixing their credit limits, and dealing with queries and collections.

The infrastructure of the Joint Credit Card Company was funded 30% each by the three main banks (Lloyds, Midland and NatWest) and 10% by The Royal Bank of Scotland/Williams & Glyn's Group. There was a complex formula for charging processing costs to the participating banks with a discount to those with above average volume and a surcharge to those below. In addition the non–shareholders such as the Bank of Ireland were charged a fee which reflects the need to recoup some of the setting–up costs from them. Each bank individually funded its own customers' credit–taking and received its own merchants service charge.

Trustee Savings Banks

In 1978, TSB Trustcard Limited, was established by the TSB Central Board to launch 'Trustcard' and became a member of VISA International. Due to the costs involved in setting–up and administering the system, Trustcard was originally administered by Barclaycard although their agreement did not preclude Trustcard from recruiting its own traders and charging different rates of interest. In October 1983 Trustcard announced their intention to break away from Barclaycard and administer their own cards and achieved its own operation based in Brighton in little over twelve months.

'T and E' cards

Although Barclaycard and Access can be used as 'charge cards', assuming the cardholder has the necessary credit limit, a separate market in 'T and E' cards has been established by three main companies whose signs can be seen at many hotels, restaurants, garages and shops: American Express, Diners' Club and Carte Blanche.

American Express started operations in the United Kingdom in the 1960s and during the next decade its sterling cardholders increased from 40,000 in 1970 to 1.1m in 1993. Income is obtained from the initial enrolment and annual subscription fees charged to cardholders and the service charge paid by traders. No extended credit is available, with cardholders paying off their balances at the end of each month. American Express is part of a multi–million dollar world–wide organisation and although its UK operations are viewed as a profit centre, the network of dealers established in this country is also part of the international acceptability of the American Express card.

Diners' Club has not shown much growth and in 1993 had 300,000 card holders. Through its subsidiary Cardholders Services Limited, it has administered several other schemes for organisations such as Trust House Forte, Post Hotels and Budget Rent–a–Car.

Carte Blanche International is a wholly–owned subsidiary of Citibank and is chartered in the State of Delaware. Carte Blanche Limited was formed in 1966 to recruit traders (mainly in London) to accept the cards of overseas visitors. There are no United Kingdom cardholders.

Eurocard

Eurocard was formed to enable the Swedish company Finansierings A Vendor to expand from their existing Kopskört and Rikskört domestic operations. By 1968 thirteen European countries had a Eurocard affiliate and Eurocard joined with the Interbank Card Association (now MasterCard) in that year. Eurocards are essentially charge cards and were originally designed for business use. Germany proved to be the major user country but now Eurocard is expanding quite quickly in Spain and elsewhere. Of course, Eurocard and eurocheque merged in the 1990s to form Europay International S.A.

International

The international development of credit cards has been dominated by VISA International and MasterCard.

The international acceptability of VISA and MasterCard has not been plain sailing. In 1981, for example, the Australian banks terminated their agreements with both although several major Australian banks subsequently rejoined MasterCard. In Europe, the opposition has been led by Dr Eckart van Hooven of Deutsche Bank of West Germany whose disagreements with Dee Hock, the then President of VISA International, attracted much publicity. In 1968, fifteen European banks joined the eurocheque system (symbolised by the blue and red letters 'EC'). It was not until May 1983 that the first British bank (Midland) joined the eurocheque system. A rival to the eurocheque appeared when the National Girobank issued Postcheques which can be cashed at 80,000 post offices across Europe. In 1990 MasterCard reached a partnership agreement with Eurocard – now Europay – which helped meet some of the reluctance of certain continental banks to MasterCard, and, indirectly, VISA.

The eurocheque system

The world money transmission systems have been dominated in the United States, Europe and the rest of the free world by the development of the VISA and MasterCard systems. However, in Europe there has been a reluctance to fully absorb systems into systems seen as being dominated by the USA. In particular, the German banks have wanted to maintain the personal customer relationship, which they feel might be threatened by the impersonal nature of electronic banking.

Europe has experienced a boom in foreign tourism for both holidays and business purposes. 80% of all foreign tourists live in a few highly industrialised countries in the Western world. 50% of all income from world tourism comes to Europe. On average foreign currency income from tourism is 6% of GDP although Spain is as high as 18%.

The eurocheque system was set up in 1968. Previously the main form of currency transfer was via letters of credit, very much for the wealthy customer. As tourism increased several key needs arose such as availability of funds, simplification of transactions and removal of the need to make funds available in advance. These requirements coincided with the development of consumer banking. Also in Europe, industrial companies were encouraging the movement away from payment of wages by cash to cheque or credit transfer and thus more individuals were opening bank accounts. A number of banks issued cheque cards and a series of bilateral agreements developed as various banks arranged reciprocal agreements in other countries.

On 10 May 1968 following a German initiative there was a meeting of representatives of banks in 15 countries at the Deutsche Bank in Frankfurt. Although the individuals were keen to establish a common system, there was a clash between those countries which had developed cheque guarantee cards and those who favoured credit cards. It proved impossible to reach agreement and a second conference was called on 17/18 October 1968 in Paris. The eurocheque name was established and the blue and red EC Symbol agreed. Countries were divided into one of two categories: those issuing and accepting cheque guarantee cards (active countries) and those only accepting them (passive countries). Inauguration of this scheme took place on 1 May 1969. In 1972 a uniform eurocheque and a uniform eurocheque card were introduced into Benelux countries, and Germany and Finland. From 1975 the cheques could be written in the currency of the host country.

The eurocheque system is Europe's largest payment method. An early warning system to cover fraud has been established with each country having one financial institution acting as an early warning station. The principal competition is from the charge cards, American Express, Diners' Club and Eurocard. The UK clearing banks as a group have stayed out of the agreement, (perhaps because of their memberships of VISA and MasterCard). However Midland Bank became a participant in the eurocheque system and now other UK banks issue eurocheques.

Eurocheques have watermarks and are generally less easy to forge than traditional UK cheques. Eurocheque merged with Eurocard to form Europay International S.A. in 1992.

APPENDIX THREE:

A CREDIT CARD AGREEMENT FORM

The example credit card agreement form on
pages 144-147 is reproduced by kind permission of
Save and Prosper Group Limited, London.

CREDIT AGREEMENT REGULATED BY THE CONSUMER CREDIT ACT 1974

ROBERT FLEMING ⬦ **SAVE & PROSPER**

SAVE & PROSPER GROUP LIMITED,
BANKING ADMINISTRATION CENTRE,
FREEPOST, ROMFORD RM1 1BR

VISA/MASTERCARD APPLICATION
Please use capitals throughout, answer all questions and tick boxes as requested.

ABOUT WHERE YOU LIVE

Address...

....

....

....Postcode...................

Do you own the above property? ☐ Yes ☐ No

Type of Residence ☐ House (Detached) ☐ House (Semi-Detached) ☐ Flat
☐ House (Terraced)

Number of bedrooms.....................

Council Tax Band ☐ A ☐ B ☐ C ☐ D ☐ E ☐ F ☐ G ☐ H

Period at present address.................years

If at present address less than three years ☐
or
If address of property owned is different from above ☐
(Please tick box as appropriate)

Please give address of property below:

....

....

....

....Postcode...................

ABOUT YOU

Title/Mr/Mrs/Miss ....Surname.................

First Name(s)...

Date of Birth...

MARITAL STATUS ☐ Married ☐ Single ☐ Divorced/Separated ☐ Widow(er)

Number of Dependants.................

Existing Save & Prosper/Robert Fleming Account Number (if any).................

National Insurance Number ☐☐☐☐☐☐☐

Home Telephone (STD Code).................(Number).................

ABOUT THE SECOND APPLICANT (if applicable)

Title/Mr/Mrs/Miss.................Surname.................

First Name(s)...

Date of Birth.................Relationship to First Applicant.................

Employer's Name and Address.................

Position.................Time with employer.................years

Gross Annual Salary £.................Other Income £.................

ABOUT YOUR BANK

Name of your Bank.................

Address.................

....Postcode...................

Sort Code (as on cheques) ☐☐☐

Current Account Number.................Time with Bank.................years

ABOUT WHAT YOU DO

ARE YOU? ☐ Employed ☐ Self-Employed ☐ Unemployed ☐ Retired ☐ Student ☐ Other (please specify).................

IF EMPLOYED

Employer's Name and Address.................

....

....

Business Telephone: (STD Code).................(Number).................

Nature of Employer's Business.................

....

Position held.................

Paid ☐ Monthly ☐ Weekly   Is your position pensionable? ☐ Yes ☐ No

Time with present employer.................years

If with present employer less than three years, please give name and address of previous employer.

....

Time with previous employer.................years

IF SELF-EMPLOYED

Business Name and Address.................

....

....

Business Telephone: (STD Code).................(Number).................

Nature of Business.................

Time Self-Employed.................years

If less than three years, please give previous business name and address
or name and address of previous employer (if any).

....

....

Time with previous employer.................years

ABOUT YOUR ACCOUNT

Account Required (Tick one box only)

☐ VISA only ☐ Dual VISA and MasterCard Account

Payment Date Required

☐ Between 1st and 7th of month

☐ Between 8th and 14th of month

☐ Between 15th and 20th of month

☐ Between 21st and 24th of month

☐ Between 25th and 31st of month

Credit Limit Required

£ ....(Normally not more than 10% of your gross annual income)

Do you wish to receive information on other products and services offered by Save & Prosper and Robert Fleming?

☐ Yes ☐ No

DOCUMENTS REQUIRED

Please send us the originals of the following documents, otherwise we regret we cannot progress your application.

The documents will of course be treated as completely confidential and will be returned to you. Photocopies are not acceptable.

☐ **Proof of Home Ownership** (Most recent Mortgage statement)

☐ **Proof of Income**
(P60 for last financial year, or last salary slip. Self-Employed please send accountant's confirmation of last three years' profits)

☐ **Last three months'** statements of your main bank account.

PLEASE READ THE FOLLOWING STATEMENTS AND SIGN BELOW

Please issue a Save & Prosper/Robert Fleming VISA Card/MasterCard to me/us.

I/We have read the section entitled "Right of Cancellation" and confirm that no oral statement of the type mentioned has been made in my/our presence.

I/We confirm that the information given is true and complete.

I/We confirm that I/we have received a copy of the Save & Prosper/Robert Fleming Credit Card Rules and agree to be bound by them (as they are amended from time to time).

I/We authorise Save & Prosper and Robert Fleming to make such enquiries and take up such references as they deem necessary in connection with this application.

I am/We are both aged 18 or over.

JOINT APPLICANTS ONLY:

We confirm that you may accept the signature of either of us as authority for any transaction on the account.

We hereby waive our statutory right to receive two separate statements of account and request that statements be sent to the first-named applicant.

SIGNATURE(S) OF APPLICANT(S)

This is a Credit Agreement regulated by the Consumer Credit Act 1974.

SIGN IT ONLY IF YOU WANT TO BE LEGALLY BOUND BY ITS TERMS.

Signature of First Applicant...

Signature of Second Applicant ....

Date(s) of Signature(s) ....

ABOUT YOUR FINANCES

Your Income

Gross Annual Salary/Pension $ ....Other Income $.................per annum

Please specify source of other income:

....

Your Home

Year Property Purchased ....Purchase Price $.................

Current Mortgage Outstanding $ ....Estimated Current Value $.................

Monthly Mortgage Payments $ ....

Name of Lender...

Address of Lender ....

....Account/Roll Number ....

Details of any other property owned

Address	Current Value	Mortgage Outstanding

CREDIT COMMITMENTS

It is important you complete this section in full. You may be prosecuted for making a fraudulent application for credit if you do not give full details of all credit commitments.

Other Credit Cards: Please list all credit cards or payment cards held.
(VISA, ACCESS, MasterCard, American Express, Diners Club, Storecard, etc).

Name of Card	Amount Owing	Monthly Payments

Hire Purchase or Other Loans

Name of Lender	Amount Owing	Monthly Payments

Other Regular Commitments (e.g. Child Maintenance) $ ....per month

INFORMATION YOU NEED TO KNOW

RIGHT OF CANCELLATION

The Consumer Credit Act contains special provisions to deal with agreements concluded after a person acting for Save & Prosper/Robert Fleming & Co Limited (including possibly a supplier of goods or services) had made an oral statement in your presence about the Save & Prosper/Robert Fleming VISA/MasterCard facility. In such cases, you would have a limited right to cancel the agreement and we would have to use a different form of agreement. We cannot therefore consider your application on this form if such a statement has been made.

BE SURE YOU CAN AFFORD THE REPAYMENTS BEFORE ENTERING INTO A CREDIT AGREEMENT.

DO NOT WRITE HERE

Application accepted, and Agreement signed and executed on behalf of Save & Prosper/Robert Fleming & Co Limited.

Credit Limit £.................................. Date.................

Authorised Signature ....

P.H.O. ☐

P.I. ☐

St. ☐

10359 4/94

Both applicants to sign in event of joint application. Please ensure documents specified above are included with your application.

SAVE & PROSPER/ROBERT FLEMING 1993 CREDIT CARD RULES
This is a Credit Agreement regulated by the Consumer Credit Act 1974

Issued by: Robert Fleming & Co Limited, Banking Administration Centre, Sovereign House, 16-22 Western Road, Romford RM1 3LB.

IMPORTANT – YOU SHOULD READ THE FOLLOWING CAREFULLY BEFORE APPLYING and be sure that you can afford the repayments before entering into a Credit Agreement.
The information given in this agreement will remain applicable for at least seven days from issue.

YOUR RIGHTS

The Consumer Credit Act 1974 covers this agreement and lays down certain requirements for your protection which must be satisfied when the agreement is made. If they are not, Flemings cannot enforce the agreement against you without a court order.

The Act also gives you a number of rights. You have a right to settle this agreement at any time by giving notice in writing and paying off all amounts payable under the agreement. If you have obtained unsatisfactory goods or services under a transaction financed by this agreement apart from any purchased out of a cash loan, you may have a right to sue the supplier, Flemings or both. Similarly, if the contract is not fulfilled, perhaps because the supplier has gone out of business, you may still be able to sue Flemings.

If you would like to know more about the protection and remedies provided under the Act, you should contact either your local Trading Standards Department or your nearest Citizens' Advice Bureau.

MEANING OF WORDS AND PHRASES

1. In these Rules:
(i) *"Account"* means any account maintained by Flemings under these Rules in relation to Transactions;
(ii) *"the Agreement"* means the agreement between Flemings and the Cardholder (or, if applicable, each Cardholder) the terms of which are these Rules as varied from time to time;
(iii) *"APR"* means Annual Percentage Rate of Charge;
(iv) *"Business Day"* means any day other than Saturday, Sunday or bank holidays as defined under the Banking and Financial Dealings Act 1971;
(v) *"Card"* means either a Save & Prosper/Robert Fleming VISA Card and/or MasterCard issued in respect of an Account;
(vi) *"Cardholder"* means any person in whose name an Account is maintained, whether alone or jointly with another individual;
(vii) *"Card Payment"* means any payment made by use of a Card, Card number, PIN or authorised for debit to an Account;
(viii) *"Cash Advances"* means any cash advance obtained by use of a Card, Card number, PIN or authorised in any manner whatsoever by the Cardholder for debit to an Account;
(ix) *"Banking Administration Centre"* means the Save & Prosper/Flemings Banking Administration Centre, Sovereign House, 16-22 Western Road, Romford RM1 3LB (Telephone: 0708-766966);
(x) *"Credit Limit"* means the maximum debit balance permitted on the relevant Account from time to time;
(xi) *"Flemings"* means Robert Fleming & Co. Limited, its successors and assigns;
(xii) *"Joint Account"* means an Account maintained in the name of two persons;
(xiii) *"PIN"* means the Personal Identification Number issued for use in conjunction with a Card;
(xiv) *"Save & Prosper"* means Save & Prosper Group Limited, its successors and assigns;
(xv) *"Service"* means the Save & Prosper/Robert Fleming credit card service provided by Flemings under the terms of the Agreement;
(xvi) *"Statement"* means the statement of the relevant Account from time to time issued by or on behalf of Flemings;
(xvii) *"Transaction"* means any Card Payment or Cash Advance or, if Flemings has agreed to maintain under these Rules more than one Card

issued under the Agreement, any Card Payment made or Cash Advance obtained by use of a relevant Card;
(xviii) *"Unauthorised Transaction"* means any Transaction effected by a person who obtained possession of a relevant Card without the Cardholder's consent;
(xix) Where the context permits, words denoting the masculine gender only include the feminine gender and references to the singular include the plural;
(xx) The headings in the Agreement are for ease of reference only and do not affect the interpretation or construction of the Agreement.

FLEMINGS

2. Flemings provides the Service as principal. Flemings has authorised Save & Prosper to act as its agent to market and administer the Service. Flemings may at all times disclose to Save & Prosper, any authorised credit reference agency and any supplier of computer system services in respect of the Service details of the financial affairs of any Cardholder (including but without limitation) details of the Account.

Flemings and Save & Prosper may send any Cardholder information on any other products marketed by any member company of the Flemings Group if the Cardholder has given his consent to their doing so. A company is a member of the Flemings Group if it is a subsidiary of Robert Fleming Holdings Limited.

THE CARD

3. The only person who may use a Card is the Cardholder to whom Flemings has sent it. A Cardholder must sign his Card in ink immediately upon receipt and use it only in accordance with and subject to the Agreement.

THE ACCOUNT

4. (a) Flemings may debit the Account with the amounts of all Transactions including Unauthorised Transactions up to the limit stated in Clause 5(c) and any expenses incurred by Flemings arising from the enforcement of its rights under these Rules). The Cardholder will be liable to pay Flemings all amounts so debited whether or not a sale or cash advance voucher is signed by a Cardholder.

(b) The amount of any Transaction in a currency other than sterling will be converted at a rate of exchange decided by Flemings for the date when the Transaction is debited to the Account.

SECURITY

5. (a) A Cardholder must exercise all possible care to ensure the safety of any Card issued to him and to stop it being used by anyone not authorised by Flemings to use it. A Cardholder must keep secret the PIN which Flemings has issued to him to use with a Card. He must destroy the notice Flemings sends him of his PIN as soon as he receives it and keep any note of his PIN away from the Card to which it relates and in such a way that it cannot be identified as relating to that Card.

(b) If a Card is lost or stolen or a PIN is disclosed to any person who is not authorised by Flemings to receive such disclosure, the Cardholder must immediately notify the Banking Administration Centre. This notification may be given verbally by telephoning the Banking Administration Centre between the hours of 9.00 a.m. and 5.00 p.m. on any Business Day on 0708 766966 or, outside these hours, of the VISA Card, the VISA Travel Service Centre, London; telephone number: 071-938-1091, or in respect of a MasterCard, First Data Resources Limited; telephone number: 0702 362988. But any such verbal notification will be ineffective unless its confirmation in writing is received by the Banking Administration Centre within seven days

thereafter. The Cardholder must also immediately report the loss or theft of a Card to the police.

(c) Until Flemings receives effective notice of the loss or theft of a Card or the unauthorised disclosure of a PIN, the Cardholder (or, if the Card relates to a Joint Account, each Cardholder, jointly and severally) is liable for all Unauthorised Transactions up to a maximum of £50. Once Flemings receives effective notice, subject to Rule 12(b) below, the Cardholder's (or, if the Card relates to a Joint Account, each Cardholder's) liability for subsequent Unauthorised Transactions will end.

(d) If a Card is lost or stolen, the Cardholder (or, if the Card relates to a Joint Account, each Cardholder) must give all reasonable help to recover it. If a PIN is disclosed to any unauthorised person, the Cardholder (or, if the PIN relates to a Joint Account, each Cardholder) must give Flemings all relevant information about the unauthorised disclosure.

USE OF A CARD

6. A Cardholder:
(a) May use his Card only to obtain the facilities and the services from time to time made available by Flemings in respect of it;
(b) Must not use his Card outside the validity period shown on the Card or after any notification of withdrawal or cancellation of the Card given by Flemings or any person acting on behalf of Flemings;
(c) In using his Card to withdraw cash, may not (when aggregated with the withdrawals of any Cardholder jointly liable in respect of the Account) withdraw more than £500 on any one day;
(d) In using his Card, must comply with all the applicable exchange control regulations in force from time to time and will be held responsible for any infringement of any exchange control regulations.

THE CREDIT LIMIT

7. A Cardholder may only use his Card within the Credit Limit. This will be such amount as Flemings from time to time decides and notifies to him. If the Account is a Joint Account, the Credit Limit applies to the Cardholders jointly. In calculating whether the Credit Limit has been exceeded, full account will be taken of (i) any Transaction not yet debited to the Account; and (ii) any authorisation given by or on behalf of Flemings to a third party in respect of any prospective Transaction.

THE STATEMENT

8. Flemings will normally prepare and send a monthly Statement to the Cardholder unless there has been no movement in the Account in the relevant month. The Cardholder must examine each statement of account and tell Flemings in writing of any errors in it within thirty days of the date of the particular statement or as soon as reasonably practicable thereafter. Flemings is not liable in respect of any errors not so notified to it.

PAYMENT

9. (a) The Cardholder must ensure that there is paid within twenty-five (25) days after the date of the Statement not less than 5% of the total amount shown on the Statement to be due to Flemings, or £5, whichever is the greater (or the full amount due if this is less than £5).

(b) The Cardholder must also pay immediately all outstanding sums in excess of the Credit Limit, all arrears of previous payments, together with the amount of any Transaction entered into in breach of the terms of the Agreement.

(c) All payments hereunder made by cheque must be effected by cheque drawn in sterling on a bank in the United Kingdom, Channel Islands or the Isle of Man.

DIRECT DEBIT

10. (a) The Cardholder will have the facility, by agreement with Flemings, to use a variable direct debit charged to a current account with a bank in the United Kingdom to pay each month the minimum amount required under 9(a) above. Such direct debit payment will be made 10 days after the date of the relevant Statement.

(b) If the Cardholder cancels or otherwise varies the direct debit authority in respect of this facility, Flemings will levy a charge of £5 payable on the date of the next Statement.

(c) If any direct debit authority is dishonoured for any reason whatsoever, all sums then due on the Account will become payable forthwith unless otherwise agreed by Flemings.

CHARGES

11. (a) The Cardholder must pay an annual fee of £12 (debited yearly in advance). The annual fee may be changed at Flemings discretion.

(b) Interest will be charged on a daily basis on the balance outstanding on the date of the Statement from that date until any repayment is credited to the Account, and thereafter on such reduced balance up to and including the date of the next Statement. If, however, the whole of the balance outstanding at the date of any Statement is repaid by the close of business on the 25th day following that date, no interest will be charged on that balance.

(c) In addition to any interest charged under (b) above, if, when a Statement is issued (or the Account is closed under Rule 16 (b) below), the balance outstanding on the Account as at the date of the previous Statement has not been settled in full, interest will be charged on each Transaction made since that previous Statement, such interest to accrue on a daily basis from the date the particular Transaction took place to the date of the next Statement after the date the particular Transaction took place.

(d) Interest under (b) or (c) above will be charged at a rate of 0.95% per month (equivalent to an APR of 13.9% for Card Payments and an APR of 15.4% for Cash Advances). However, the rate of interest may be varied.

(e) A charge of 1.5% of each Cash Advance (subject to a minimum charge of £2.00) will be debited to the Account at the time when the Cash Advance is debited to the Account.

(f) Any payment made by the Cardholder to Flemings will only be effective when it is credited to the Account and will be applied in the following order: first, in payment of all interest, fees and other charges levied by Flemings; secondly, towards repayment of all Cash Advances outstanding from previous Statements; thirdly, towards Card Payments outstanding from previous Statements; fourthly, towards Cash Advances shown on the current Statement; fifthly, towards Card Payments shown on the current Statement; sixthly, towards Cash Advances not yet shown on any Statement; and seventhly, towards Card Payments not yet shown on any Statement.

(g) The Cardholder will be liable for any loss or cost which Flemings determines it has suffered as a result of any breach of the Agreement by a Cardholder and such loss or cost may be debited to the Account.

(h) Flemings may debit an Account with the sum of £5 each month if, during that month, a Cardholder has failed to make payment by the due date.

(i) Flemings may debit an Account with the sum of £5 each month if, during that month, a Cardholder has exceeded the Credit Limit.

(j) Flemings may debit an Account with the sum of £10 each month if, during that month, any settlement payment has been dishonoured.

(k) Flemings may charge the Cardholder £15 (or such other sum as Flemings decides) for obtaining and sending to the Cardholder at his request a voucher in respect of any Transaction.

(l) Flemings may charge the Cardholder £2 for issuing a duplicate statement of account.

(m) Flemings may charge the Cardholder £25 for replacing a lost or stolen Card.

LIABILITY AND REFUNDS

12. (a) Subject to (b) below, Flemings will bear the full losses incurred (i) if a Card is misused before the Cardholder receives it; (ii) if the Cardholder

suffers direct loss as a result of any fault in the machines or other systems used in connection with a Card unless the fault was obvious or advised by a message or notice on display.

(b) Flemings' liability for any loss the Cardholder may suffer in connection with a Card is limited to those amounts wrongly charged to the Account and any interest on those amounts. In any event, the Cardholder and, if the Card relates to a Joint Account, each Cardholder, jointly and severally, will be liable for all losses resulting from the Cardholder's (or, in the case of a Joint Account, either or both Cardholders') fraud or gross negligence.

(c) For the avoidance of doubt it is confirmed that Flemings will not be liable for any refusal to accept or honour a Card. If a supplier issues a refund voucher in respect of a Transaction, Flemings will credit the Account with the amount of the refund only upon the date of receipt by Flemings from VISA International or MasterCard (as appropriate) of the relevant refund voucher properly issued.

If a supplier becomes liable to make a refund but a properly issued refund voucher is not received by Flemings, subject to any statutory rights of the Cardholder, Flemings will not be liable to credit the Account with the amount of the refund and no claim by a Cardholder against the supplier will be the subject of set-off or counter-claim against Flemings. No rights of any Cardholder against Flemings may be Assigned or otherwise disposed of.

CHEQUE GUARANTEE

13. The Card does not carry a cheque guarantee facility of any kind, and must not be used by a Cardholder to guarantee payment of any cheque.

OWNERSHIP OF CARDS

14. All Cards issued under the Agreement will at all times remain the property of Flemings. Flemings may at any time without notice withdraw authorisation to use a PIN and/or a Card (without thereby affecting the Cardholder's liability in respect of such use) and require the immediate return of a Card. A Card must be returned to Flemings upon demand and may be retained by Flemings or by any person acting on behalf of Flemings.

RE-ISSUE

15. Flemings may at any time without notice refuse to re-issue, renew or replace any Card but, subject thereto, normally will issue a new Card before expiry of the validity period shown on that Card.

TERMINATION

16. (a) Flemings may at any time without notice terminate the Agreement (but without thereby affecting the Cardholder's liability in respect of use of a Card (if any)) by returning to Flemings all Cards issued under the Agreement for use on the Account, accompanied by a written request for such termination. Such termination will only take effect upon receipt of all such Cards by Flemings, together with the payment of all liabilities of the Cardholder in respect of the Account.

But if an Account is a Joint Account, such termination will take effect when Flemings receives a written request from at least one Cardholder requesting termination of the Agreement.

(b) Flemings may at any time close an Account either with immediate effect, if a Cardholder breaches the Agreement, or otherwise upon giving seven days written notice to the Cardholder (or each Cardholder if the Account is a Joint Account). In that event, the entire outstanding balance on the Account (including Transactions not yet debited thereto) will become due and payable forthwith.

(c) The Cardholder who cannot remain liable (or, if the relevant Account is a Joint Account, each Cardholder will remain liable, jointly and severally) for all Transactions on an Account whether made before or after the Agreement terminates.

THE AGREEMENT

17. (a) The Cardholder (and, if applicable, each of them) agrees on behalf of himself and his successors and personal representatives to be bound by the Rules.

This agreement with Flemings is made at Sovereign House, 16-22 Western Road, Romford RM1 3LB.

(b) If any provision in these Rules is illegal or unenforceable, the remainder of these Rules will remain in full force and effect.

GOVERNING LAW

18. These Rules are governed by English Law.

AMENDMENT

19. Flemings may change these Rules at any time on giving the Cardholder reasonable notice, such notice to be given by letter or message on the Cardholder's statement of account or advertisement in two UK national newspapers, as Flemings considers appropriate. Seven days notice will be given of any change in the rate of interest charged. For the purpose of these Rules, notice given by post will be deemed to be received forty-eight hours after the time of posting.

FORCE MAJEURE

20. Flemings will not be liable if it is unable to perform its obligations under the Agreement by reason (directly or otherwise) of any industrial dispute, equipment or computer failure, or any cause outside the control of Flemings. If Flemings is unable to produce or send any statement, the Cardholder's liability for interest will continue.

CHANGE OF ADDRESS

21. The Cardholder will immediately notify the Banking Administration Centre in writing in the event of any change of name and/or address. If Fleming believes that there is any doubt about the address at which the Cardholder resides, Flemings may refuse to authorise Transactions (without liability for any consequences of doing so) until the Cardholder's address is confirmed to Flemings' satisfaction.

JOINT ACCOUNTS

22. If an Account is a Joint Account:

(a) Flemings may accept the signature of either Cardholder as authority for any Transaction and, if either Cardholder should die, Flemings may accept the signature of the survivor as authority for any Transaction or other dealing with the Account;

(b) the liability of each Cardholder is joint and several and any obligations of a Cardholder under the Agreement is binding on each of them;

(c) Flemings may accept the instructions (written or verbal) of either Cardholder in relation to an Account.

BANKRUPTCY OR DEATH

23. (a) On the bankruptcy or death of any Cardholder his obligations will remain in full force and effect until such time as they are fully satisfied. On the bankruptcy or death of a Cardholder any joint Cardholder must immediately inform Flemings of such occurrence and return the Card(s).

(b) Subject to any statutory limitation, all sums due under the Agreement are payable in full immediately if any Cardholder becomes bankrupt or dies.

BENEFITS

24. Any facility or benefit provided or otherwise made available to a Cardholder in respect of an Account may be withdrawn at any time without notice.

LOSS OR MISUSE OF A SAVE & PROSPER/ROBERT FLEMING VISA CARD OR MASTERCARD

If a VISA and/or MasterCard is lost, stolen or misused by someone who obtained it without your consent, you may be liable for up to £50 of any loss to Flemings in respect of the Card. If it is misused with your permission you will probably be liable for ALL losses. You will not be liable for losses to Flemings which take place after you have told Flemings of the theft, etc, provided you confirm any oral message in writing within seven days.

February 1994　　　　10359 4/94

APPENDIX FOUR:

A MERCHANT AGREEMENT FORM

The example merchant agreement form on
pages 150-151 is reproduced by kind
permission of Barclays Bank PLC.

FOR OFFICE USE ONLY

A _____   E _____

B _____   F _____

C _____   G _____

D _____   H _____

BARCLAYS MERCHANT SERVICES AGREEMENT

THIS AGREEMENT is made the   day of   19

BETWEEN

(1) BARCLAYS BANK PLC (registered no. 1026167) of 54 Lombard Steet, London EC3P 3AH ("Barclays Merchant Services") and

(2) _____

(registered no. _____) of _____

_____ (VAT no. _____) ("the Merchant").

I/WE HAVE READ AND AGREE TO BE BOUND BY THE TERMS AND CONDITIONS OVERLEAF.

BARCLAYS BANK PLC

By _____

    AUTHORISED SIGNATORY

THE MERCHANT

By _____ _____ _____

    AUTHORISED SIGNATORY   NAME   POSITION

Please write in block capitals below the full names of (all) Proprietor / Partners / Directors

SURNAME   FORENAME(S)   SURNAME   FORENAME(S)

_____ _____ _____ _____

_____ _____ _____ _____

_____ _____ _____ _____

             (continue on a separate sheet if necessary)

Schedule

1. Merchant Service Charge:

    Visa

    _____ on each UK debit card transaction

    _____ on the value of all other Card transactions

    MasterCard

    _____ on each UK debit card transaction

    _____ on the value of all other Card transactions

    _____

    _____

2. Initial Fee:

    £ _____

    All charges exclusive of Relevant Tax.

3. Floor Limits:

    Card Transactions where the Cardholder is present   £ _____

    Card Transactions where the Cardholder is not present   £ _____

    _____   £ _____

    _____   £ _____

19600 06/93   MA3

This Agreement sets out the terms on which the Merchant will accept Cards as a means of payment and on which Card Transactions will be authorised by and presented to Barclays Merchant Services.

IT IS AGREED as follows:

1. Definitions

1.1 As used in this Agreement:

"this Agreement" includes the Schedule and any operating instructions and/or procedure guides which Barclays Merchant Services may notify from time to time and with which the Merchant shall comply;

"Card" means any valid financial service card (including any debit or credit card) approved by Barclays Merchant Services from time to time;

"Cardholder" means the individual for whose use a card has been issued at any time;

"Card Refund" means any refund given in respect of a Card Transaction for credit to the Cardholder's account;

"Card Refund Data" means details of a Card Refund in a form approved by Barclays Merchant Services;

"Card Transaction" means any payment made or (if permitted by a procedure guide) cash advance obtained by the use of a Card, a Card number or in any manner authorised by the Cardholder for debit to the Cardholder's account;

"Card Transaction Data" means details of a Card Transaction in a form approved by Barclays Merchant Services;

"Floor Limit" means the total value of the sales (as notified from time to time) that the Merchant may make to a Cardholder on any one occasion without Barclays Merchant Services' authorisation;

"Relevant Tax" means any value added tax or any other similar tax or duty;

"United Kingdom" includes Channel Islands and Isle of Man.

1.2 The headings are inserted in this Agreement for convenience only and shall not effect its construction.

1.3 If the expression "the Merchant" comprises more than one person the liability of such persons under this Agreement shall be joint and several.

1.4 This Agreement is governed by English law and both parties shall comply with all legislation applicable to them as a result of this Agreement. Any payments hereunder are due in sterling and financial limits specified in sterling shall be observed by the Merchant in the corresponding amount of any relevant foreign currency.

2. Barclays Merchant Services' obligation

Barclays Merchant Services will;

2.1 pay to the Merchant the amount of all Card Transactions effected and presented in accordance with the terms of this Agreement by crediting a bank account nominated by the Merchant within the United Kingdom;

2.2 send the Merchant statements showing for the statement period:

2.2.1 the value of Card Transactions processed by Barclays Merchant Services; and

2.2.2 the amount of service charge plus any Relevant Tax and any other sums due to Barclays Merchant Services under this Agreement.

3. Merchant's obligations

3.1 (a) Subject to paragraph (b), the Merchant will honour all Cards presented by accepting them as a means of payment and, where relevant, by supplying goods, services or other facilities on the same terms (other than price) as they are supplied for cash.

(b) If the Card is of a type specified in any operating instruction and/or procedure guide, the Merchant must only charge the Cardholder the cash price.

3.2 In accordance with the relevant procedure guide, the Merchant will:

3.2.1 obtain authorisation from Barclays Merchant Services at the time of and for a particular Card Transaction if a Cardholder requires goods, services or other facilities for an amount;

(a) in excess of the Floor Limit; or

(b) falling within a range notified to the Merchant from time to time;

3.2.2 contact Barclays Merchant Services immediately to cancel an authorisation if the sale in respect of which the authorisation was obtained is not thereupon concluded;

3.2.3 present Card Transaction Data and Card Refund Data to Barclays Merchant Services, or such other person as is approved by Barclays Merchant Services, within 3 banking days of the relevant Card Transaction or Card Refund (together (if relevant) with cash or a cheque for the amount by which Card Refunds exceed the value of Card Transactions presented) and the presentation of Card Transaction Data shall be a warranty that the goods, services or other facilities have been supplied;

3.2.4 on the instructions of and as directed by Barclays Merchant Services retain any Card presented;

3.2.5 in any case other than sub-clause 3.2.4, not act, nor purport to act as agent of Barclays Merchant Services. If the Merchant is deemed agent of Barclays Merchant Services by statute, the Merchant shall immediately send to Barclays Merchant Services any notice received from a Cardholder.

3.3 The Merchant will not:

3.3.1 honour a Card in order to provide cash (unless permitted by a procedure guide) nor where the provision of credit is unlawful;

3.3.2 supply any other person with equipment to enable them to effect Card Transactions nor present to Barclays Merchant Services Card Transaction Data which was not originated as a result of a transaction between a Cardholder and the Merchant.

4. Charge-back Rights

4.1 Barclays Merchant Services may withhold payment on presentation of Card Transaction Data or, if the Merchant has been paid for the Card Transaction, charge-back the amount of the Card Transaction to the Merchant if:

4.1.1 Card Transaction Data is issued or presented in breach of this Agreement (which includes any operating instruction or procedure guide); or

4.1.2 a Cardholder makes a claim relating to a Card Transaction;. or

4.1.3 the Merchant fails to produce, at Barclays Merchant Services' request, evidence of the Cardholder's authority to debit the amount of a Card Transaction in the form approved by Barclays Merchant Services or the Cardholder denies having authorised a telephone order; or

4.1.4 any circumstance specified in a relevant procedure guide as entitling the Bank to make a charge-back occurs; or

4.1.5 any circumstance specified in sub-clause 4.2 occurs, or Barclays Merchant Services considers it is likely to occur, and the goods services or other facilities referred to in the Card Transaction Data have not yet been supplied.

4.2 The events referred to in paragraph 4.1.5 are:

4.2.1 the presentation of a petition to wind up the Merchant or to appoint an administrator of the Merchant;

4.2.2 the convening of a meeting of members of the Merchant to consider and if thought fit pass a resolution for the voluntary winding up of the Merchant;

4.2.3 the appointment of a receiver over any material part of the property or undertaking of the Merchant;

4.2.4 the making of any proposal in respect of the Merchant for a composition in satisfaction of debts or a scheme of arrangement (formal or informal); or

4.2.5 the death of or the presentation of a bankruptcy petition against the Merchant or the making of an application for an interim order pursuant to Section 253 of the Insolvency Act 1986 in respect of the Merchant.

4.3 The amount of any Card Transaction which Barclays Merchant Services is entitled to charge-back to the Merchant under this Agreement shall be a debt immediately due from the Merchant to Barclays Merchant Services.

4.4 If, under this Agreement, Barclays Merchant Services withholds payment on any Card Transaction Data or the amount of any Card Transaction Data is charged-back to the Merchant, Barclays Merchant Services shall be under no responsibility to procure payment for the Card Transaction or otherwise deal with the Cardholder in respect thereof and the Merchant shall not re-present in any manner Card Transaction Data relating to such Card Transaction.

5. Charges

The Merchant will pay the charges (plus Relevant Tax) specified in the Schedule in consideration of the provision by Barclays Merchant Services of Services under this Agreement. Barclays Merchant Services may vary the rate or basis of its charges on giving not less than one month's written notice.

6. Promotion of the Cards

The Merchant shall adequately display at each premises the promotional sign(s) or other material provided by Barclays Merchant Services and may use names or designs approved by Barclays Merchant Services solely to indicate that Cards are accepted for payment. The Merchant shall not use any other material referring to Barclays Merchant Services or any other name associated with Cards without Barclays Merchant Services' approval.

7. Barclays Merchant Services' Property

Barclays Merchant Services equipment lent to Merchants in connection with this Agreement will remain Barclays Merchant Services' property and will be returned to it on request.

8. Indemnities

The Merchant shall indemnify Barclays Merchant Services against all losses, costs, penalties, payments or liabilities whatsoever arising out of

(a) any claim being made or defence raised against Barclays Merchant Services by a Cardholder where such a claim or defence is a direct or indirect result of any act or omission on the part of the Merchant which includes, but is not limited to, the act of supply; and

(b) any breach of this Agreement including breaches of any procedures and instructions resulting in additional work for Barclays Merchant Services.

9. Cardholder Disputes and Fraud Prevention

9.1 The Merchant will take all reasonable steps to assist Barclays Merchant Services in handling a claim by a Cardholder against Barclays Merchant Services. Barclays Merchant Services shall have complete discretion whether or not to defend any such claim or to negotiate any settlement with the Cardholder which shall be binding on the Merchant.

9.2 The Merchant will provide Barclays Merchant Services with reasonable assistance requested from time to time for the prevention and detection of fraud and will inform Barclays Merchant Services of any material change in the nature or size of its business which, if not notified to Barclays Merchant Services, might suggest fraudulent activity at the Merchant.

10. Set-off

Barclays Merchant Services may set off the amount of any liability incurred by the Merchant to Barclays Merchant Services under this Agreement or, if any of the events specified in sub-clause 4.2 occurs, in any other manner whatsoever, against any sum which would otherwise be due to the Merchant from Barclays Merchant Services, whether under this Agreement or otherwise. If Barclays Merchant Services considers that the Merchant is likely to incur any such liability, it shall not be obliged to make any payment of sums which would otherwise be due to the Merchant hereunder until either the liability is incurred when Barclays Merchant Services will pay the balance of such sums to the Merchant after deducting the amount of any such liability, or Barclays Merchant Services is satisfied that no such liability will be incurred or if incurred Barclays Merchant Services will be reimbursed promptly by the Merchant.

11. Force Majeure

Barclays Merchant Services shall not be under any liability if it is unable to perform its obligations due directly or indirectly to the failure of any machine, data processing system or transmission link or to industrial dispute, or to anything outside the control of any of Barclays Merchant Services, its agents and sub-contractors.

12. Direct Debit

The Merchant will authorise the Merchant's bank to pay on presentation all requests for payment of a direct debit initiated by Barclays Merchant Services in respect of amounts due to Barclays Merchant Services under this Agreement.

13. Interest on Late Payments

Any sum due to Barclays Merchant Services under this Agreement shall be immediately payable. Barclays Merchant Services may charge interest at the rate of 2% per month on a daily basis whether before or after judgment on any sum which the Merchant fails to pay. Interest accrued shall be payable at the end of each month.

14. Confidentiality

14.1 The Merchant shall not:

14.1.1 compile or use any lists of Cardholders or Card numbers or any other information relating to Barclays Merchant Services' business (which includes any information contained in the Schedule) except for the purpose of this Agreement; nor

14.1.2 disclose any such information to any third party apart from a professional advisor or agent or sub-contractor appointed under Clause 17 or where required or permitted to do so by law.

14.2 The Merchant agrees Barclays Merchant Services may use any Card Transaction Data for any purpose whatsoever provided that Barclays Merchant Services shall not (unless required or permitted to do so by law) disclose any confidential information in respect of such Data or any other confidential information about the Merchant, its business or customers outside the Barclays' Group without the Merchant's consent in writing.

15. Variation

Subject to clause 5, Barclays Merchant Services reserves the right to vary or amend the terms of this Agreement on notice to the Merchant.

16. Termination

16.1 This Agreement shall terminate upon:

16.1.1 either party giving notice to the other; or

16.1.2 the occurrence of any of the events specified in sub-clause 4.2 and the Merchant shall notify Barclays Merchant Services as soon as it becomes aware that any such event is likely to occur or has occurred.

Immediately upon the occurrence of any of the events referred to in paragraph 16.1,1 and 16.1.2 Card Transaction and Card Refund Data shall be presented to Barclays Merchant Services, Northampton, NN1 1SG within three banking days of the Card Transactions or Card Refunds effected or given.

16.2 Termination shall not affect obligations already incurred and Clauses 4, 7, 8, 9, 12, 13, 14, 17 and this Clause shall remain in effect.

17. Assignment and Appointment of Agents and Sub-contractors

This Agreement is not assignable by the Merchant [but in the case of individuals shall bind their personal representatives]. Any agent or sub-contractor appointed by the Merchant to implement any of the terms of this Agreement shall be approved by Barclays Merchant Services in writing and Barclays Merchant Services may withdraw its approval at any time. If Barclays Merchant Services approves any agent or sub-contractor then the Merchant shall be responsible for ensuring that such agent or sub-contractor observes the relevant terms of this Agreement, in particular, the terms of Clause 14 and references to the Merchant shall be deemed to include references to such agents or sub-contractors.

18. Waiver

No waiver by Barclays Merchant Services of any breach of this Agreement shall operate as a waiver of any subsequent or continuing breach. If any of the events specified in sub-clause 4.2 occur and for any reason Barclays Merchant Services does not treat this Agreement as terminated at that time, Barclays Merchant Services shall still be entitled to treat this Agreement as terminated at any later date without being obliged to give the Merchant notice of termination and, until such time, the Merchant shall continue to observe, and be bound by, the terms of this Agreement.

19. Notices

Any written notice may be sent by first class post to the last known place of business or registered office of the Merchant or in the case of Barclays Merchant Services to Barclays Merchant Services, Northampton, NN1 1SG and shall be deemed to have been received by the addressee at noon on the second business day after posting (excluding the day of despatch).

20. Existing Merchant Agreement

Any existing Merchant Agreement and any supplemental agreement or other agreement between Barclays Merchant Services and the Merchant to similar effect shall terminate immediately on the execution of this Agreement except in respect of accrued rights.

Commission 133
private:
 health care plans 21
 label card 127
Profile Points 21, 54
Provident & Clothing Supply
 Company 135-6

Quotations Regulations 91

Race Relations Act (1976) 81
Regulation Z 132
repayment programmes, credit cards 13
retail stores 36, 121
retailer cards see store cards
retailers *see* **merchants**
Royal Bank of Scotland 31-2, 50,
 92, 137-8

sales vouchers 127
Save & Prosper 14, 55-6, 63, 71, 117-18
 agreement forms 143-8
Schneider, Ralph 129
secured card facilities 119
security 111, 138
Sex Discrimination Act (1975) 81
Signa cards, Coutts & Co. 15
Signet 31, 33
Interbank Card Ass'n 134
Single Market 119-20
smart card *see* **Integrated Circuit Card**
South East Bankers Association 131
staff 115
 training 112
Standard Chartered Bank 20
stockmarket crash (1987) 61
store cards 16, 34-5, 45, 81, 127
 value of transactions 45
stores 36, 121

Sunday Times, VISA card 15
supplier see merchants
Switch 16, 46, 51, 127
 membership of Consortium (1993) 47
Switch system 50

technology 103-8
telecommunications 107, 120
telephone cards 17, 127
TMS Corporation of the Americas 133
traders see merchants
transactions 134
 processing 112-13
Travel & Entertainment (T & E)
 cards 129, 131, 138-9
travellers' cheques 19-20
Trustcard 111
Trustee Savings Banks 137-8
Truth in Lending Simplification
 & Reform Act (1980) 132-3
types of cards 13
 average transactions *42*
 average turnover *41*

UK:
 building societies 110
 clearing banks, eurocheque
  system 140-1
 economy 25
 market 117-19
  statistics 39-48
unfair contracts 120-1
Unfair Contracts Terms Act (1977) 81
United California Bank 130
US, domestic expansion 132

Valley National Bank 130
VISA cards 13, 27-9
 cash advancements 99